BY WHAT AUTHORITY?

BY WHAT AUTHORITY?

WILLIAM BARCLAY

Judson Press
Valley Forge

●

First published in Great Britain 1974
by Darton, Longman and Todd Ltd
85 Gloucester Road, London SW7 4SU

© 1974 William Barclay

Published in 1975 by
Judson Press, Valley Forge, PA 19481

Library of Congress Cataloging in Publication Data

Barclay, William, lecturer in the University of
  Glasgow.
    By what authority?

  1. Authority (Religion)—History of doctrines.
I. Title.
BT88.B35   201.1   75-4532
ISBN 0-8170-0675-3

Printed in the U.S.A.

CONTENTS

Chapter 1

Authority in the Old Testament
The Authority of the Spirit

Our subject is authority, and we will do well to begin by trying broadly to define what authority is. To have authority is to have the right to make statements and demands, and to act, by personal right, and without consulting anyone or anything else. To put it very simply, to have authority is to have the right to choose and to settle one's own course of action without consulting anyone else, and to have the right to tell people what to do and what not to do, what to believe and what not to believe on one's own personal responsibility.

We shall later have to think about the authority of Jesus, but we may note here and now that it is these very things which gave Jesus his characteristic note of authority.

When the people listened to him, 'The crowds were astonished at his teaching for he taught them as one who had authority and not as their scribes' (Matthew 7. 28, 29). The scribes were the experts in the Law. But the characteristic of the scribes was that no scribe ever made a statement on his own. He would give an opinion, but he would back it up with the words, 'There is a teaching that...' He would cite an array of witnesses, and call as evidence the words of this or that scribe who agreed with him. As we might put it, the scribes tended to speak in footnotes. When Jesus spoke, he spoke as if his words needed no support other than that he said them. That is the accent of authority.

When Jesus made demands, he offered no justification for making them other than that he made them. For the Jew the Law was the most sacred and divine and binding thing in the world, but Jesus could and did say: 'You have heard that it was said ... But I say to you ...' (Matthew 5. 22, 28, 32, 34, 39, 44). It was enough that he said it. Even if we take it that Jesus was not so much contradicting as explaining the Law, even if we take it that the sense is: 'This is what the Law says; I now tell you what it means', it is still true that Jesus is claiming the sovereign right to interpret and to restate the Law, without reference to anyone else's verdict or opinion. That again is the accent of authority.

When Jesus acted, he offered no justification for his action, other than the fact that he chose to do it. When he banished the money-changers and the sellers of sacrificial victims from the Temple courts, the Jews asked him what right he had to act like that – and in the end he never told them (Matthew 21. 23–27; Mark 11. 27–33; Luke 20. 1–8; John 2. 18–22). No one *gave* him the right to do this astonishing thing; he acted as if he personally possessed the right. That is the action of authority.

When we look at authority in general, we find that almost always authority is exercised within a certain sphere. A man can be an authority on playing the piano and no authority at all on playing golf. A man may be an authority on Latin and Greek; he may be an authoritative classicist; but he may have no authority at all in nuclear physics; his ignorance in science may be as great as his expertise in classics.

From this it is clear that at least in part authority is based on knowledge. If I wish to erect a building that will stand up, I have to accept the authority of an architect, who has knowledge of the laws by which buildings are constructed. If I wish to have an illness cured, I must accept the authority of the doctor, who knows the laws of health. If I am involved in a legal problem, I must accept the authority of the lawyer, who has knowledge of the laws. Clearly, knowledge and authority are closely inter-related.

So far so good – but it is nothing like the whole way. There is more to authority than knowledge. A man might be an entirely competent architect, and yet not be able to create a building which men will come to see. A man may have a faultless knowledge of anatomy, and yet not be a great surgeon. A man may be able to pass any examination in the law, and yet be neither a great pleader nor a great judge. A man might be festooned with degrees in education. and yet be a disaster in the classroom. Henri the Fourth of France said of James the Sixth of Scotland and the First of England that he was 'the wisest fool in Christendom'. He had vast stocks of learning and little equipment in sense.

And nowhere is this more true than in the realm of religion. Julian Duguid in his book *I am persuaded* tells how in boyhood days he looked at clergymen. They had the right training; they had gone to the right college or university or seminary; they had the right degrees; they had the right clerical clothing. But there was more to it than that. Somehow they seemed to him tired and hair-splitting. It matters because as Julian Duguid says: 'Children do not think in theories; they argue from personali-ties.' So he goes on to say: 'The fact remains that, to this day, I am critical when faced with clergymen. My first reaction is not: "Here is a man of God: let me refresh myself in his knowledge", but: "Is he in touch with God? Does he know, or even believe, the magnificence of what he preached"'. The knowledge was there all right, but not the authority.

But later in life Julian Duguid had the very opposite experience. It was on his first visit to America. 'I was introduced at Victoria Station,' he writes, 'to a small, lithe, tough-set man, very wiry and quiet on his feet. For a week on board the *Aquitania* his face astonished and held me: I had never experienced such power. His skin had been weathered and wrinkled by the storms of the northern coasts. His hair was grey and upright, and he was not what the world calls young. Yet, he had an aura of peace and strength which could be felt across the smoking-room. With hundreds of strangers present, and my own back turned, I could tell directly he entered.' The name of the man in question was Wilfred Grenfell, Grenfell of Labrador, the Labrador doctor. And this man exuded authority like a kind of human electric current.

Here then is the essence of authority in a person. It is usually limited to one sphere. Duguid said of an old Somerset game-keeper: 'He knew to a hair what he knew, and never pontificated beyond it.' Within his sphere he had authority. Authority is based on knowledge, and for the simplest of all reasons – a man must know what he is talking about. But knowledge is not in itself enough to beget or confer authority. Beyond the knowledge there must be the mystery of a human personality, a personality which is somehow something plus – and in due time we shall try to see whence the plus comes.

It is authority in religion with which for the moment we are concerned. There is a clear sense in which religion and authority must go hand in hand. The most probable derivation of the word *religion* is from the Latin verb *religare*, which means *to bind*. This is to say that in religion there are certain beliefs and actions which are *binding*. Religion *binds* a man to a way of belief and a way of life. In it there must therefore be those to whom the binding elements are revealed, and those whose function it is to see that the binding things are accepted and observed.

So now we turn to the first area in which we are going to look at this matter of authority, the area of the Old Testament.

From the beginning of their history as a nation one

recurring demand of God was the basis of Hebrew religion:

'I am the Lord your God; consecrate yourselves, therefore, and be holy for I am holy ... I am the Lord who
brought you out of the land of Egypt, to be your God;
you shall therefore be holy, for I am holy' (Leviticus 11.
44, 45).

'And the Lord said to Moses, "Say to all the congregation of the people of Israel, You shall be holy, for I the
Lord your God am holy"' (Leviticus 19. 1, 2).

'Consecrate yourselves, therefore, and be holy; for I am
the Lord your God' (Leviticus 20. 7).

'You shall be holy to me; for I the Lord am holy' (Leviticus 20. 26).

It is of primary importance to understand what this
word *holy* means in this context. To modern ears the idea
that the word *holy* conveys is the idea of saintliness, of
special goodness, of the odour of sanctity, of – to put it
pictorially – stained-glass windows. A holy man to us is
rather a man detached from life, removed from the common ways, whose *habitat* is the church, or the religious
community, or the hermit's cell rather than the shop or
the factory or the office or the market-place. But that is
not the basic meaning of the word either in Hebrew
(*kadosh*), or in Greek (*hagios*). In Hebrew and in Greek
the idea of the word *holy* is the idea of difference, of
separation from ordinary things. The Sabbath day is holy
because it is different from other days. The Bible is holy
because it is different from other books. The communion
and the communion table are holy because they are
different from other meals and from other furniture. A
priest is holy because he is set apart from ordinary men.
And God is supremely holy because God is supremely the

'wholly other'. This comes out quite clearly in the Old Testament. The last quotation we made from Leviticus is incomplete. Let us complete it:

> 'You shall be holy to me; for I the Lord am holy, and have separated you from the peoples, that you should be mine' (Leviticus 20. 26).

For Israel, holiness involved separation; it meant that they must be different from the other peoples and the other nations of the world. About them there had to be something 'other'.

And now another supremely important piece has to be added to this pattern. This difference, this separation has to be expressed not in withdrawal from the world, but in involvement in the world. The difference is to be expressed not in separation from the world in the sense of leaving the world, but by living in the world in obedience to a way of life and belief which is different from that of those who do not recognise or accept God.

> 'The Lord will establish you as a people holy to himself, as he has sworn to you, if you keep the commandments of the Lord your God, and walk in his ways' (Deuteronomy 28. 9).

The difference is to be expressed not in detachment from but in involvement in the world. It is not in some religious community that the Jew had to be different, but in the life and work of the world. He was to be different not by living in a stained-glass-window sphere but in the market-place.

It is just here that the idea of authority makes its entry. If this difference is so necessary, there must be someone to say what the difference is, someone continually to confront people with it, someone to remind them if they forget, to rebuke them if they stray, to stimulate and inspire them, if they grow weary. In the Old Testament there are two kinds of authority which do just that. First.

there is the authority of the Spirit, and the authority of the Spirit is located in the prophets, and in the rest of this chapter it is at that authority that we will look. In regard to the prophets two questions emerge. First, where did they get their authority? What was the source of it? Second, what was the area in which their authority acted? In what spheres did they claim to tell men what they must do, and what they must refrain from doing?

First, then, whence came the prophetic authority? It is here that our previous discussion on the sources of authority becomes relevant. Clearly, the prophets did not possess what we would now call a professional training and an academic qualification for their job. Their qualification was much more personal than that.

The basis of the prophetic qualification was an experience. In one way or another the prophets began with a direct experience of God. In many cases they tell us of that experience. In each case the experience was different. What we might call the authorising experience of God came to very different men in very different ways, and the differences are very significant.

Isaiah, says J. E. McFadyen, was the most regal of the prophets. In all probability Isaiah was an aristocrat. He had familiar access to kings. He came to Jerusalem to speak to Ahaz (Isaiah 7. 1–9). He was clearly the familiar friend of Hezekiah (Isaiah chapters 36–39; 2 Kings 20. 1–19). Isaiah was the aristocrat to whom kings were friends and the court familiar territory. Further, it was in the Temple that Isaiah had his vision and his call. 'I saw the Lord sitting upon a throne, high and lifted up; and his train filled the Temple.' It was in the Temple, when his lips had been touched with the burning coal from the altar, that Isaiah responded with his: 'Here am I! Send me' (Isaiah 6). The vision came to him in 740 B.C. and his work lasted until 701 B.C.

Isaiah was the aristocrat to whom God spoke in the splendour of the Temple in Jerusalem. The Jewish schol-

ars even found grounds for believing that Isaiah was of
royal blood. He is said to be the son of Amoz (Isaiah 1. 1).
It was suggested by some imaginative Jewish scholar that
Amoz comes from the root *'amas*, which means to be
mighty, and which occurs again in the name of Amaziah
the king. So on such a slender foundation is built the
theory that Amoz the father of Isaiah and Amaziah the
king were brothers and that therefore Isaiah was of the
royal line.

Jeremiah's call came to him in 626 B.C. Jeremiah belonged to a line of priests, and he came from the village
of Anathoth (Jeremiah 1. 1). There were far too many
priests to serve all at the one time; they were divided into
twenty-four courses or sections, each of which served,
apart from the great festivals like Passover, Pentecost and
Tabernacles, for only two weeks in the year, and Anathoth was one of the villages which had been given to the
priests in which to reside, when they were not on Temple
duty (Joshua 21. 18). Clearly, Jeremiah would have been
happy to have remained in peaceful Anathoth; to him his
call and his vision were a disturbance (Jeremiah 1. 4–8).

So Jeremiah was a priest living the protected life of a
priest, and it may well be that his experience came to
him, not at the court and not in the Temple, but in some
quiet garden, whose peace he loved.

'And the word of God came to me saying: "Jeremiah,
what do you see?" And I said: "I see a rod of almond."
Then the Lord said to me: "You have seen well, for I
am watching over my word to perform it"' (Jeremiah
1. 11, 12).

A strange passage – what was the point of the vision?
The point lies in a play on words in the Hebrew which is
not translatable into English. The word used for *almond*
is an unusual, and a poetical word. The almond has been
likened to the snowdrop, for it blossoms when other trees
are still asleep. So sometimes it was called *shaked*, which

means *that which is awake*. Then God says to Isaiah: 'I am *watching*,' and the word for watching is *shoked*, which comes from the same root as *shaked* and closely resembles it. So in the garden Jeremiah saw the almond, awake when the other trees slept, and it reminded him of the God who is awake, on the watch, the God who neither slumbers nor sleeps, in regard to his purposes.

So we have the difference. Isaiah was the aristocrat to whom the vision came in the reverent splendour of the Temple. Jeremiah was of priestly lineage, and God spoke to him in the quiet peace of a garden, whose peace he must leave to become the mouthpiece of God's authority to men.

Let us move to still another of the prophets, to Amos, who was thundering out his message of doom to the lush civilisation of the Northern Kingdom about the years 765 to 750 B.C. Amos was one of the shepherds of Tekoa (Amos 1. 1). 'I am no prophet,' he says, 'nor a prophet's son; but I am a herdsman, and a dresser of sycamore trees, and the Lord took me from following the flock, and the Lord said to me: Go prophesy to my people Israel' (Amos 7. 14, 15). Amos had no special qualifications at all. He did not belong to the priestly class, as Jeremiah did. He did not enjoy aristocracy of birth, as Isaiah did, for to be a dresser of sycamore trees was one of the humblest occupations on which a man could engage. Amos was one of the people.

It was not in the Temple that his vision came to him, and it was not in some quiet garden. Although the work of Amos was done in the Northern Kingdom, Tekoa was in Judea on the very edge of the desert, which men called the Desolation. As George Adam Smith said of Amos, he had 'the shepherd's horror of the extravagances and the cruelties of civilisation'. As Harper said in his commentary on the book of Amos, Tekoa looked out on a desolate, dreary and savage world, an unmitigated wilderness. It was an environment abounding in emptiness and stillness. In such an environment Amos was able to develop the power of observation and reflection, the austere habits of the recluse, and the unpitying sharpness of the censor of his country's faults and vices. It was in the bleak, open spaces, alone with the wind and the sun and the stars, that Amos, neither aristocrat nor priest, the extraordinary ordinary man saw his vision, received his call, and heard his message from God.

Here again is the difference. Isaiah is the aristocrat; Jeremiah is the priestly youth; Amos is the technically uneducated man from the wide open spaces. Isaiah found his vision in the Temple, Jeremiah in the garden, Amos in the desert places. They were very different men and in very different places they had their authorising vision of God.

We have still another prophet to include in this varied company. Hosea's work was done from 743 to 733 B.C. We know nothing about him personally. But we do know that his call and his message came to him through a domestic tragedy.

Hosea married a woman called Gomer, and she was one of these women who somehow or other are born to be unfaithful, a fact which God knew but which at first Hosea did not know. He had a son called Jezreel, and at the time he did not know that the child was not his son. So his wife became a prostitute. She had another girl baby, who was not Hosea's, and Hosea called her No-Love; and then a boy baby of whom again Hosea was not the father, and Hosea called him Not-my-kin. The woman left home, and she became a slave-concubine to some man. But the trouble was that, do what she liked, Hosea could not stop loving her. So even then he bought her back at the price of a slave, and she came home (Hosea 1. 1–3. 4).

And what had happened to him with Gomer taught Hosea something, for it came to him: 'If I a man cannot stop loving the woman who strays again and again, if I cannot shut my heart to her, if I must always take her back and back and back, how much more must God in his love never stop loving his people, however often they stray away? Gomer could break my heart, but she could not break my love. And, if it is that way with me, how much more so with God?' Hosea in his domestic tragedy found his call and his message.

Isaiah the aristocrat, Jeremiah the priest, Amos the workman, Hosea the family man – in the splendour of the Temple, in the peace of the garden, in the austerity of the desert, in the life of the family – the authorising vision came to many kinds of men in many kinds of circumstances.

So then the authority of the prophet springs from a direct experience of God, an experience which is not confined to one kind of person, nor to one kind of place. But it has to be noted that this experience is not the end of the matter. The experience is the beginning of a continuing contact with God. No one can fail to see how the writings of the prophets are punctuated by the ever-recurring phrase: 'Thus says the Lord.' To the prophet God is not only the One who spoke; God is also the One who speaks. We may therefore say that the source of the prophetic authority is an initial experience of God and a continuing contact with God.

We have now to illustrate the spirit and define the message of this prophetic authority. We must begin with some explanation of the method by which we do so. Clearly, most of our material must be taken from the prophets themselves, but we will also draw largely from Deuteronomy and to some extent from Proverbs, and we must ask why it is justifiable, and indeed essential, to use these books to throw light on the mind and the material of the prophets.

J. E. McFadyen called Deuteronomy 'one of the epoch-making books of the world'. Most Old Testament scholars would agree that the story in 2 Kings 22–23. 3 tells of the

finding of the book of Deuteronomy. In the eighteenth
year of the good king Josiah, Shaphan the secretary of
state was sent to the Temple to carry out certain financial
arrangements. He was thereupon informed by Hilkiah
the priest: 'I have found the book of the law in the house
of the Lord.' The book was taken by Shaphan and read
to Josiah. Josiah was stricken in heart and conscience by
the conviction of the need for the reformation of the
national religion, and by the threat of the wrath of God.
So the book was read to the people, and king and people
together entered into a covenant to serve and to obey
God. It can therefore be said that in a very real sense the
book of Deuteronomy is the foundation document of
Judaism.

If we accept this view of the discovery and the impact
of Deuteronomy, what was it that gave it its special importance and impact? No one will deny the greatness of
the prophets, but there is a sense in which the prophets
were ineffective. First, as R. H. Pfeiffer says, a prophet
like Amos was too revolutionary for general acceptance.
He was prophesying in a day when 'the nation had pretty
well discarded conduct for cult', and his message demanded such a revolution that it shattered rather than
attracted. Second, Amos had said, as all the prophets had
said in one way or another: 'Let justice run down as
waters, and righteousness as a mighty stream' (Amos 5.
24). But, as R. H. Pfeiffer puts it, righteousness for Amos
was 'merely a principle'; it needed definition, and it is
precisely that definition that Deuteronomy gives it.
Righteousness became in Deuteronomy the keeping of
the statutes and the ordinances which the Lord their God
had given them (Deuteronomy 6. 1, 2). J. E. McFadyen
develops this view: 'Deuteronomy rendered a great service to religion by translating its large spirit into demands which could be apprehended of the common
people. The book is splendidly practical, and formed a
perhaps not unnecessary supplement to the teaching of

the prophets. Society needs to have its ideals embodied in suggestions and commands, and this is done in Deuteronomy. Doubtless the prophets had done the deepest thing of all by insisting on the new heart and the return to Jehovah, but they had offered no programme of practical reform. Just such a programme is supplied by Deuteronomy.' If the word be allowed, Deuteronomy is the 'practicalising' of the message of the prophets – and that is why no book has a better claim to be used to illustrate the prophetic teaching.

But we have no sooner said that than it becomes necessary to say something else. What we have said might be interpreted to mean that Deuteronomy turns the prophetic idealism into unprophetic legalism, that the prophetic principles have become the Deuteronomic laws. Nothing could be further from the truth, because in Deuteronomy the one dynamic of action is love to God. J. E. McFadyen says that the programme offered by Deuteronomy 'is saved from the externalism of being merely a religious programme by its tender and uniform insistence upon the duty of *loving* Jehovah with the whole heart'. R. H. Pfeiffer says that 'for the Deuteronomist, as for Hosea, love for God is the essence of true religion' (Deuteronomy 6. 5). S. R. Driver writes of Deuteronomy: 'Duties are not to be performed from secondary motives, such as fear, or dread of the consequences; they are to be the spontaneous outcome of a heart penetrated by an all-absorbing sense of personal devotion to God.' Of this love three things are to be said.

i. It is founded on memory. 'You shall remember' runs like an ever-recurring theme through Deuteronomy. They are to remember how they were brought out of Egypt; they are to remember what God did to Pharaoh; they are to remember the night they left Egypt; above all they are to remember that they were servants and slaves and that God redeemed them (Deuteronomy 5. 15; 7. 18; 15. 15; 16. 3, 12). 'Remember what God did for you – and

you cannot help but love' – that is the basic message of
Deuteronomy.

ii. It issues in obedience. 'You shall love the Lord your
God with all your heart, and with all your soul, and with
all your might. And these words which I command you
this day shall be upon your heart' (Deuteronomy 6. 5, 6).
God is 'the faithful God who keeps covenant and steadfast love with those who love him and keep his commandments' (Deuteronomy 7. 9). 'And now, Israel, what
does the Lord your God require of you, but to fear the
Lord your God, to walk in all his ways, to love him, to
serve the Lord your God with all your heart and with all
your soul, and to keep the commandments and statutes of
the Lord?' (Deuteronomy 10. 12, 13). 'You shall therefore
love the Lord your God, and keep his charge, his statutes,
his ordinances and his commandments always' (Deuteronomy 11. 1; cp. 11. 13, 22). God will bless and prosper
them 'provided you are careful to keep all this commandment, which I command you this day, by loving the Lord
your God and by walking ever in his ways' (Deuteronomy
19. 9; cp. 30. 6, 16, 20). Remember – love – obey – these
are the dominant notes of the Deuteronomic demand.

iii. This obedience founded on love means something
else. It means that an act of obedience is an act of rejoicing. 'You shall rejoice before the Lord your God' – that is
the instruction when offerings are brought, when the
Passover is celebrated, when the Feast of Weeks is kept,
all through the Feast of Tabernacles, when the first fruits
are brought (Deuteronomy 12. 12, 18; 16. 1–8; 9–12;
13–15; 26. 10, 11). The obedience of love is not duty; it is
joy.

So then we may well use Deuteronomy to illustrate the
reach of the prophetic authority, because Deuteronomy is
the book which provides a programme for prophecy, and
a programme in which memory produces love, and love
produces obedience, and obedience produces joy.

The other book from which we draw material to illus-

trate the scope and the substance of the prophetic authority
is Proverbs, which like Deuteronomy is not directly
a prophetic book. Proverbs is a specimen of what is called
the Wisdom Literature. The Wisdom Literature in the
Old Testament includes Proverbs, Job, Ecclesiastes, and
certain of the Psalms, Psalms 1, 37, 49, 73, 91, 126. Outside the Old Testament the most famous Wisdom books
are the apocryphal books. The Wisdom of Jesus the Son of
Sirach, or, as it is commonly called, Ecclesiasticus. The
Wisdom Literature is the work of the wise men, or, as we
might call them, The Sages of Israel.

There are traces of these Sages far back in Jewish history. We find at the court of the kings an official whom
the A.V. calls the scribe, and whom the R.S.V. calls the
secretary, in the sense of the secretary of state. So we read
of David's staff: 'Joab the son of Zeruiah was over the
army; and Jehoshaphat the son of Ahilud was recorder;
and Zadok the son of Ahitub and Ahimelech the son of
Abiathar were priests; and Seraiah was secretary; and
Benaiah the son of Jehoiada was over the Cherethites and
Pelethites (that is, over the king's bodyguard of Philistine
mercenaries)' (2 Samuel 8. 16–18; cp. 2 Samuel 20. 25;
1 Kings 4. 3; 2 Kings 19. 2; Jeremiah 36. 20, 21). The narrative in 2 Kings 22. 3–13 shows how important a part
Shaphan the secretary of state played in the discovery
and the proclaiming of Deuteronomy.

These secretaries were men of mature wisdom. They
had often travelled and seen the world, and they were
often wealthy and used to good living. It has even been
suggested that there was a school for training them. In
Joshua 15. 15, there is mentioned Kiriath-sepher, which
literally means Book City; in the Septuagint, the Greek
translation of the Hebrew Old Testament, this city appears
as the City of the Scribes. (In Hebrew this would require
the change of only one letter – Kiriath-sopher instead of
Kiriath-sepher.) So it has been suggested that this was the
city where the scribes or secretaries were trained. But in

Joshua 15. 49 the same town is called Kiriath-sannah, which means the City of the Palm Leaf. In those ancient days the palm leaf was the writing material of the scribe, and it is more likely that this city, called in the Hebrew the City of the Book, or the City of the Palm Leaf, was the depot and the main producer of writing material.

However that may be, these sages were important people in the administration of the nation. By the time we reach Jeremiah these Wise Men, or Sages, as they had come to be called (*hakamim* in Hebrew, in which wisdom is *hokmah*), have come to form a class like the prophets and the priests. We read in Jeremiah (18. 18) 'The law shall not perish from the *priest*, nor counsel from the *wise*, nor the word from the *prophet*.' How then do these Sages fit in with the prophets, and in what way are they related to them? What was this wisdom? What did it teach and what did it offer?

i. By far the most characteristic feature of this wisdom was that it was intensely practical. It was never, or extremely rarely, speculative or philosophic. If it ever did become speculative and philosophic, it was under Greek influence. Let us then see what this practical wisdom included.

Traditionally, Solomon was the wisest man who ever lived (1 Kings 4. 29-34). It was wisdom which made Solomon successful in his diplomatic relations with Hiram of Tyre (1 Kings 5. 12). It was his wisdom which made Solomon able to come to the correct decision in the dispute about which woman the child belonged to (1 Kings 3. 16-28). It was wisdom which enabled Solomon to answer the hard questions with which the Queen of Sheba tested him (1 Kings 10. 1-3). It was wisdom which made Solomon an expert on the trees and the plants and the animals (1 Kings 4. 33, 34). It was wisdom which gave the wise woman of Tekoa her shrewdness (2 Samuel 14. 1-24). It was the wisdom of the wise woman which saved Abel of Beth-maacah from massacre at the hands of Joab and his men (2 Samuel 20. 14–22). It is a man discreet and wise whom Pharaoh needs as the food-controller of Egypt, as Joseph tells him (Genesis 41. 33). It is wise men whom Moses needs and chooses to share the responsibility of leadership with him (Deuteronomy 1. 13).

All kinds of crafts come from wisdom. It is wisdom which gives skill in the making of garments (Exodus 28. 3); the fashioning of idols (Isaiah 40. 20); the construction of furniture for the Tabernacle (Exodus 31. 6, 7); the ability to spin (Exodus 35. 25). It is wisdom which makes the wailers at mournings skilful in leading lamentation (Jeremiah 9. 17). It is wisdom which makes a man shrewd, cunning, crafty (2 Samuel 13. 3; Job 5. 13). It is wisdom which makes men good pilots at sea (Ezekiel 27. 8), or gives them the ability to charm snakes (Psalm 58. 5). It is wisdom which equips the little animals with their instincts and their ability to survive:

> Four things on earth are small,
>   but they are exceedingly wise;
> the ants are a people not strong,
>   yet they provide their food in the summer;
> the badgers are a people not mighty,
>   yet they make their homes in the rocks;
> the locusts have no king,
>   yet all of them march in ranks;
> the lizard you can take in your hands,
>   yet it is in kings' palaces (Proverbs 30. 24–28).

There is a kaleidoscopic quality in this wisdom, which equips a man for any situation in life. W. A. L. Elmslie writes of this variegated wisdom: 'In one breath the Sage will warn his pupil of unjust dealing before a partner or friend, of theft in the place where he sojourns, of falsifying an oath or a covenant, and of leaning on the table with his elbow, when at meat.' Wisdom is that which equips great and small for life and living.

ii. The aim of the Sages was to enable men to live the

happy life. 'Wisdom, as ordinarily understood,' says R. H. Pfeiffer, 'is the same thing as the art of living.' J. Pedersen describes wisdom as 'a skill shaping the very thought which yields the right result'. W. O. E. Oesterley and T. H. Robinson write in their *Introduction to the Books of the Old Testament*: 'The main object of the exponents of wisdom was to teach men how to live happy lives as long as they were on this earth. This leads them to deal with the relationship between a man and his God, between parents and children, man and wife, friend and foe, rich and poor, high and low; they teach what is right behaviour in every phase and occupation of life, how to accept adverse fortune, and the fitting attitude of him who enjoys wealth – in a word how to live to the best advantage, to do right because it brings its own reward, to avoid wrong-doing because it entails disadvantages.' In general, 'wisdom is the faculty of being able to distinguish between what is advantageous and what is detrimental . To have wisdom and to have happiness and to enjoy prosperity are the same thing.

iii. It would be quite wrong to leave the matter there. To do so would be to give the impression that wisdom is no more than a mere shrewdness, an eye to the main chance, the secret of material and social success. One of the main characteristics of the wisdom literature is 'the intimate connection between ethics and religion'. For the Sages 'wisdom and piety are one and the same thing'. 'The fear of the Lord is the beginning of wisdom' (Proverbs 9. 10). To walk in uprightness is to fear the Lord (Proverbs 14. 2). The first chapter of Ecclesiasticus is a meditation on wisdom and the fear of God. 'All wisdom comes from the Lord.' 'The fear of the Lord is glory and exultation ... The fear of the Lord delights the heart ... With him who fears the Lord it will go well at the end ... To fear the Lord is the beginning of wisdom ... To fear the Lord is wisdom's full measure ... The fear of the Lord is the crown of wisdom ... To fear the Lord is the

root of wisdom ... If you desire wisdom, keep the commandments' (Ecclesiasticus 1. 1–26). The fear of the Lord
comes first. All wisdom is the fear of the Lord; wisdom is
the fulfilment of the law. 'Better is the God-fearing man
who lacks intelligence, than the highly prudent man who
transgresses the law' (Ecclesiasticus 19. 20, 24). Riches and
honour and life is the reward of the fear of the Lord
(Proverbs 22. 4). It is the name of God which is a strong
tower, and every word of God is a shield to those who
take refuge in him (Proverbs 18. 10; 30. 5). God is the
guide even of wisdom, and the corrector of the wise (Wisdom 7. 15).

Clearly, for the wisdom writers there is no wisdom
which does not have its beginning, its middle and its end
in God.

iv. Now we come directly to the connection between
prophet and sage. As Oesterley and Robinson have
pointed out, in the earliest days, before the Exile, both
prophet and priest may well have disapproved of the
sage, and the disapproval may well have been returned.
The prophets would think of the sages as lacking zeal for
God, for the sage is altogether a quieter and less flaming
personality than the prophet. The priest would resent the
coldness of the sage to the cult. The sage with what he
regarded as his superior wisdom would find the prophet
arbitrary and hard, and the priest narrow-minded and
cult-centred.

But after the Exile the prophets ceased, never in
Judaism to return; the voice of prophecy was for ever
silenced; and bit by bit any gap between the sage and the
priest narrowed. And then the supremely important
thing happened – it was precisely the prophetic message
that the sage taught and expounded. H. Ranston writes
in *The Old Testament Wisdom Books and their Teaching*: 'It is customary, and with justification, to regard the
prophets as the most illustrious exponents of the Hebrew
religious spirit. But it may be doubted if the influence of

these spiritual experts would have been so permanent
and far-reaching apart from the work of the wise men in
popularising their ideals and creating among the ordinary people a spirit sympathetic with them.' It was the
prophetic ideal which the sages were keeping alive. In
The Book that is alive John Paterson writes: 'The Sages
were the spiritual middlemen who mediated the exalted
doctrines of the prophets and interpreted them in terms
of common life and experience. They succeeded where
the prophets failed; they reached the common people.'
True, the Sages never blazed with the divine fire of the
prophets, but John Paterson writes of them: 'The Sages,
of course, do not shoot at the moon. They are marked by
moderation. They do not look for supermen, but if they
can subtract from the number of fools, and add to the
number of the wise, they will not have laboured in vain.
Their aim is one possible of attainment. No heroic ideals
are here, only sanctified common sense, moderation, tem-
perance, self-control. These find response from men as
the loftier and more inaccessible ideas and ideals of the
prophets never did.'

So then when we speak of the spirit and the area of the
prophetic authority we are right to use not only the
works of the prophets themselves but also the book of
Deuteronomy which turned the prophetic principles into
a programme for life, and a programme based not on
legalism but on love, and on the works and words which
the Sages have left us, for the Sages preserved and taught
and communicated the prophetic message, when the
voice of prophecy was silent.

There were certain basic things of which the prophets
were quite sure.

The prophets were certain that the authority which
they were exercising was not their own authority, but the
authority of God. The prophet never said: 'This is what I
say'; the prophet always said: 'This is what God says.'
The prophet was not speaking for himself; he was speak-

ing for God. He was not expressing an opinion; he was transmitting a divine command.

The prophets were nevertheless quite sure of their own place in the revealing of the authoritative pronouncements and commands of God. 'Surely,' said Amos, 'the Lord God does nothing, without revealing his secret to his servants the prophets' (Amos 3. 7). They knew themselves to be the mouthpieces through whom God spoke to men.

Whatever their message of wrath and condemnation, the prophets never doubted the special place of the Jewish nation in the purpose and in the heart of God. But to them that special place was at least as much a responsibility as it was a privilege. Amos hears God say:

'You only have I known
    of all the families of the earth;
therefore will I punish you
    for all your iniquities' (Amos 3. 2).

In popular thought the Jews often regarded their chosenness as a guarantee of exemption from punishment; as the prophets saw it, it was a reason for sterner and more severe punishment. The people thought of the privilege of being chosen; the prophet thought of the responsibility.

The prophets regarded the events of nature and of history as a series of warnings to the nation. The fact that many warnings had been sent, and had been consistently disregarded, meant a greater guilt and a greater liability to the punishment of God. One of the great passages of Amos is the passage in which God tells of the warnings he had sent – famine, drought, blight and mildew, pestilence, disaster – and in which every section ends (five times) with the refrain: 'Yet you did not return to me, says the Lord' (Amos 4. 6–11). The land, says Jeremiah, has been ruined and laid waste like a wilderness, and it has made no difference to the disobedience and the in-

fidelity of the nation. Therefore punishment is on the
way (Jeremiah 9. 12–16). 'She listens to no voice, she accepts no correction,' says Zephaniah of the nation. He
hears God say:

> 'Surely she will fear me,
>   she will accept correction;
> she will not lose sight
>   of all that I have enjoined upon her.
> But all the more they were eager
>   to make all their deeds corrupt'
>   (Zephaniah 3. 2, 7).

Haggai hears the word of God: 'I smote you and all
the products of your toil with blight and mildew and
hail; yet you did not return to me' (Haggai 2. 17). The
ancient peoples knew nothing of secondary causes. They
did not say that the storm was due to certain atmospheric
conditions; they did not say that the failure of the crops
was due to weather or soil conditions. Everything, so they
believed, was due to the direct action of God. Therefore,
history and nature were alike the voice of God. The
nation had disregarded the warnings, and so the greater
was its guilt.

Authority is the authority of God; the prophet is the
mouthpiece of God; privilege and responsibility are in-
separably connected; the world is full of the warnings of
God for those who have eyes to see; these were basic prophetic convictions. So now we look at the authority of
which the prophets spoke.

i. The authority of God knows no natural boundaries.
Amos hears God say to the people:

> 'Are you not like the Ethiopians to me,
>   O people of Israel? says the Lord.
> Did I not bring up Israel from the land of Egypt,
>   and the Philistines from Caphtor
>   and the Syrians from Kir?' (Amos 9. 7).

'In that day,' says Isaiah, 'there will be a highway from Egypt to Assyria, and the Assyrian will come into Egypt, and the Egyptian into Assyria, and the Egyptians will worship with the Assyrians. In that day Israel will be the third with Egypt and Assyria, a blessing in the midst of the earth, whom the Lord of hosts has blessed, saying, "Blessed be Egypt my people, and Assyria the work of my hands, and Israel my heritage"' (Isaiah 19. 23, 24).

This is one of the greatest affirmations of the prophets. Too often the Jewish nation had regarded their chosenness as involving the rejection of all other nations. Too often this explained their hatred of, and contempt for, the Gentiles. They sometimes claimed that, because of their connection with Abraham, they were saved from all punishment and condemnation in the world to come, simply because they were Jews. In the Mishnah tractate on the Sanhedrin it is written: 'All Israelites have a share in the world to come' (Mishnah, Sanhedrin 10. 1). It was even said that Abraham was stationed at the gates of Gehenna to turn back any Jew who might have found his way there. There were Jews who believed that they were the chosen people and that God had no use for any other nation, and that simply as Jews and descendants of Abraham they were safe from all judgment. The prophets laid it down that there was no 'most favoured nation' clause in the kingdom of God, and that the authority of God is as wide as the world.

ii. The authority of God knows no social boundaries. The highest and the lowest, the richest and the poorest, are both subject to it and protected by it. So the prophet rebuked and threatened kings as Elijah did Ahab, and Amos did Jeroboam (1 Kings 21. 17–19; Amos 7. 10). The Levites alone had no land as an inheritance (Joshua 13. 14; 14. 3, 4). Their inheritance was to come from the offerings of the people, and their rights are constantly insisted upon and preserved (Deuteronomy 12. 19; 14. 27,

29; 26. 13). The appeal of the poor must never be refused, when he wants to borrow. Every seventh year was the year of release, when debts were cancelled, and, when such a year drew near, the temptation was to refuse to lend, lest the debt be never paid. But the poor must never be refused. 'You shall open wide your hand to your brother, to the needy and to the poor, in the land' (Deuteronomy 15. 7–11). The hired servant, the day-labourer, lived always on the verge of poverty. He must be paid his wages before the day ends, 'lest he cry against you to the Lord, and it be sin in you' (Deuteronomy 24. 14, 15). The man on the lowest rung of the social and economic scale is under the protection of the authority of God. If a Hebrew is reduced to such a state of poverty that he has to sell himself as a slave, after six years' service, in the seventh year he is to be set free, and he is not to be sent away empty-handed (Deuteronomy 15. 12–15). An escaped slave is to be given sanctuary, and is not to be handed back to the master from whom he has escaped (Deuteronomy 23. 15, 16). In particular the rights of the stranger, the foreigner who has come to stay in a Jewish community, the sojourner have to be carefully guarded. He too is to share in the joy of the great festivals (Deuteronomy 16. 11, 14; 26. 11, 13); he too is to enjoy the Sabbath rest (Deuteronomy 5. 14). 'Love the sojourner therefore; for you were sojourners in the land of Egypt' (Deuteronomy 10. 19). Justice for the sojourner must never be perverted (Deuteronomy 24. 17); the man who so perverts justice for the foreigner is accursed (Deuteronomy 27. 19). As Leviticus puts it: 'You shall have one law for the sojourner and for the native' (Leviticus 24. 22).

The authority of God stretches from the king's palace to the day-labourer's hovel, from the prince to the slave.

iii. The authority of God demands a high degree of social consciousness and social justice. Isaiah hears God say:

'Cease to do evil,
　learn to do good;
seek justice,
　correct oppression;
defend the fatherless,
　plead for the widow' (Isaiah 1. 16, 17).

This is of the very essence of the message and the demand of Amos. The book of Amos has been rightly called
'a cry for justice'. Israel is condemned

'Because they sell the righteous for silver
　and the needy for a pair of shoes –
they that trample the head of the poor
　into the dust of the earth,
　and turn aside the way of the afflicted'
　　　　　　　　　　　　　　(Amos 2. 5–7).

The luxury loving matrons are unsparingly condemned:

'Hear this word, you cows of Bashan,
　who are in the mountain of Samaria,
who oppress the poor, who crush the needy,
　who say to their husbands:
　"Bring that we may drink"' (Amos 4. 1).

God's anger is on those who 'turn justice to wormwood,
and cast down righteousness to the earth' (Amos 5. 7).
God's condemnation is on those who hate reproof, who
abhor the truth, who trample upon the poor and are
guilty of extortion. They will never live in their splendid
houses; they will never drink the wine from their lush
vineyards. They take bribes, and refuse justice to the
poor. If they are to live and to escape the wrath of God
they must hate evil and love good and establish justice in
the gate (Amos 5. 10–15). The reckoning is coming to
those who lie on their ivory couches, who eat the best
lambs and calves, who make their own music, who drink
wine in bowls, and who never think of the ruin of their

country (Amos 6. 1–8). The demand that God sends
through Jeremiah is: 'Do justice and righteousness, and
deliver from the hand of the oppressor him who has been
robbed. And do no wrong or violence to the alien, the
fatherless and the widow, nor shed innocent blood in this
place' (Jeremiah 22. 2, 3). 'Let justice roll down like
waters,' says Amos, 'and righteousness like an ever-flowing
stream' (Amos 5. 24).

The authority of God demands social justice. If religion is not expressed in justice, it is not religion at all.

iv. The authority of God will never accept cult instead
of conduct. The finest ritual and the most elaborate liturgy are no substitute for ethical action. An elaborate
liturgy divorced from ethical action, social justice, the
awareness of the needs and rights of others, is an abomination to God. It is from this conviction that there come
many of the most passionate and the most moving passages in the prophets.

'What to me is the multitude of your sacrifices?
  says the Lord;
I have had enough of burnt offerings of rams
  and the fat of fed beasts;
I do not delight in the blood of bulls,
  or of lambs, or of he-goats.

'When you come to appear before me
  who requires of you
  this trampling of my courts?
Bring no more vain offerings;
  incense is an abomination to me.
New moon and sabbath and the calling of assemblies –
  I cannot endure iniquity and solemn assembly.
Your new moons and your appointed feasts
  my soul hates;
they have become a burden to me,
  I am weary of bearing them.

'When you spread forth your hands,
   I will hide my eyes from you;
even though you make many prayers,
   I will not listen;
   your hands are full of blood' (Isaiah 1. 11–15).

'With what shall I come before the Lord,
   and bow myself before God on high?
Shall I come before him with burnt-offerings,
   with calves a year old?
Will the Lord be pleased with
   thousands of rams,
   with ten thousands of rivers of oil?
Shall I give my first-born for my transgression,
   the fruit of my body for the sin of my soul?
He has showed you, O man, what is good;
   and what does the Lord require of you,
but to do justice, and to love kindness,
   and to walk humbly with your God?' (Micah 6. 6–8).

'Come to Bethel and transgress;
   to Gilgal and multiply transgression;
bring your sacrifices every morning,
   your tithes every three days;
offer a sacrifice of thanksgiving
   of that which is leavened,
   and proclaim freewill offerings,
     publish them;
for so you love to do, O people of Israel!'

                    (Amos 4. 4, 5).

In the eyes of Amos the whole sacrificial system is one vast transgression, if it is cult without conduct.

   'I hate, I despise your feasts,
      and I take no delight in your solemn assemblies.
     Even though you offer me burnt-offerings
       and cereal offerings,

I will not accept them,
and the peace-offerings of your fatted beasts
　　I will not look upon.
Take away from me the noise of your songs;
　　to the melody of your harps I will not listen.
But let justice roll down like waters,
　　and righteousness like a never-flowing stream'
　　　　　　　　　　　　　　　　(Amos 5. 21–24).

'Is not this the fast that I choose: .
　　to loose the bonds of wickedness,
　　to undo the thongs of the yoke,
to let the oppressed go free,
　　and to break every yoke?
Is it not to share your bread with the hungry,
　　and bring the homeless poor into your house;
when you see the naked to cover him,
　　and not to hide yourself from your own flesh?'
　　　　　　　　　　　　　　　　(Isaiah 58. 6, 7).

'I desire steadfast love and not sacrifice,
　　the knowledge of God rather than burnt-offerings'
　　　　　　　　　　　　　　　　(Hosea 6. 6).

'He who slaughters an ox is like him
　　Who kills a man;
he who sacrifices a lamb,
　　like him who breaks a dog's neck;
he who presents a cereal offering
　　like him who offers swine's blood;
he who makes a memorial offering of frankincense
　　like him who blesses an idol' (Isaiah 66. 3).

A sacrifice ought to be the symbolic sign of a heart of
love, a life of devotion, and a mind in which penitence is
working a godly sorrow. When it is a mere convention, an

evasion of reality, a cheap attempt to escape the consequence of sin, then it is an abomination, and it disgusts
God instead of pleasing him.

v. It might seem superfluous to say so, although we
shall soon see that there were good reasons why it was
not, the authority of God extended over temple, shrine
and priest. There were two problems in regard to worship in Palestine. First, there was the problem of the cult
prostitutes. It is said of Josiah that he broke down the
houses of the male cult prostitutes 'which were in the
house of the Lord' (2 Kings 23. 7). So there was prostitution – even male homosexual prostitution – within the
house of the Lord. It is laid down in Deuteronomy:
'There shall be no cult prostitute of the daughters of
Israel, neither shall there be a cult prostitute of the sons of
Israel' (Deuteronomy 23. 17). In the time of Rehoboam it
was part of the prevailing wickedness that 'there were
also male prostitutes in the land' (1 Kings 14. 24). Asa was
said to have removed them (1 Kings 15. 12) a process
which Jehoshaphat continued and completed (1 Kings 22.
46).

The use of the cult prostitutes was a practice which
both Amos and Hosea sternly condemned. Amos speaks
of a man and his father both going into the same maiden,
so that God's holy name is profaned (Amos 2. 7). 'Men
themselves go aside with harlots,' says Hosea, 'and sacrifice with cult prostitutes' (Hosea 4. 14). The temple and
the shrines of Palestine had an odd resemblance to
brothels.

The second charge made against the priests and the
shrines is the charge of drunkenness. Isaiah writes:

'Woe to those who rise early in the morning,
    that they may run after strong drink,
who tarry late into the evening,
    till wine inflames them!' (Isaiah 5. 11).

'Woe to those who are heroes at drinking wine,
    and valiant men in mixing strong drink!'

(Isaiah 5. 22).

'These also reel with wine
    and stagger with strong drink;
the priest and the prophet reel with strong drink,
    they are confused with wine,
    they stagger with strong drink;
they err in vision,
    they stumble in giving judgment.
For all tables are full of vomit,
    no place is without filthiness' (Isaiah 28. 7, 8).

It is an extraordinary thing that a shrine should be a cross between a public brothel and an ill-conducted tavern. There was even an attempt to corrupt and to silence the Nazirites and the prophets. Amos has it:

'But you made the Nazirites drink wine,
    and commanded the prophets,
    saying, You shall not prophesy' (Amos 2. 12).

Jeremiah talks of the men of Anathoth who threaten him with death, if he continues to prophesy in the name of the Lord (Jeremiah 11. 21).

There was a reason for all this. In the Old Testament we read much about Baal worship. Baal is not a proper name; it means Lord; and there were many baals, many lords. The worship of the people of Palestine, the Canaanites, when the people of Israel arrived there is often called Baal worship. It was in fact fertility worship. The ancient people were fascinated and awed by the power of growth, the power of life. What made the corn, and the olive, and the grape grow? What brought the earth so wondrously to life in the spring time, and what made the harvest so generous in the autumn time? Wonderful as the fertility powers of the earth are, the supreme life force is sex, the mysterious force which brings a child into the world and gives him life. The Baals were the powers of these life forces. If the life forces are divine, then to use them is to worship. To drink the wine is to worship. To engage in the sex act is to engage in an act of worship. Hence the sacred cult prostitutes, hence the drunkenness in the shrines. It is in face of this that Hosea writes of Israel in the name of God:

'She did not know
   that it was I who gave her
   the grain, and the wine, and the oil' (Hosea 2. 8).

Baal worship was a fertility cult. In such a cult to become drunk on wine and to lie with a prostitute became acts of worship. The authority of God had to cleanse religion at its very source; the shrine where men worship had to be disinfected and purified.

vi. The prophets were convinced that the authority of God should be supreme in the political sphere. Time and again the prophets played the part of politicians, especially in regard to the foreign policy of the nation. 'Everything,' said Péguy, 'begins in mysticism and ends in politics.' And the prophets would have agreed. Nothing can happen without the vision, but the vision can never become fact without the processes of politics and government. So Amos foretold the death of Jeroboam and the exile of the Northern Kingdom (Amos 7. 10, 11). So Isaiah guided the foreign policy of Hezekiah in relation to Assyria and Babylon (Isaiah 37; 39; 2 Kings 19. 20–34; 20. 12–19). So Jeremiah left no doubt about the triumph of Nebuchadnezzar and Babylon and of what the nation's attitude to the situation ought to be (Jeremiah 32–34).

Any nation which lived in Palestine was forced into politics. The trouble was that Palestine lay between two great empires, the empire of the north, whether that empire was Assyria or Babylon, and the empire of the south, which was Egypt. Whenever these two great empires came into clash or competition, Palestine was necessarily involved; and the politicians of Palestine in their foreign policy had continually to make the political gamble of lining up with the north or the south. Always the prophets entered the debate, and always their message was that the duty of the nation was not to calculate the profit or the prudentiality of this or that alliance but to do and accept the will of God. The prophets did not argue as to whether or not religion and politics were connected; they assumed it; it was the basic fact on which their message was built. He who is lord of the individual heart is lord of the nations too, and his will is to be sought and his authority accepted in the life of nations as well as in the life of men. Ideally, political action should be the concrete expression of the will of God.

vii. The prophets were certain that the authority of God should rule in the commercial world. It is an extraordinary fact that the duty of using correct and fair weights and measures is laid down, and laid down with the greatest seriousness, no fewer than six times.

'You shall have just balances, just weights, a just ephah, and a just hin: I am the Lord your God who brought you out of Egypt' (Leviticus 19. 36).

The implication is that the just weights and measures are just as important to God as the events of the exodus from Egypt.

'A false balance is an abomination to the Lord,
   but a just weight is his delight' (Proverbs 11. 1).

'A just balance and scales are the Lord's;
   all the weights in the bag are his work'
                                    (Proverbs 16. 11).

'Diverse weights are an abomination to the Lord,
   and false scales are not good' (Proverbs 20. 33).

'You shall have just balances, a just ephah and a just bath.'

Ezekiel writes, and then he goes on to define the ephah, the bath, the homer, the shekel, the gerah, the mina (Ezekiel 45. 10). Weights and measures were very much the business of the prophets. Amos condemns those who

'make the ephah small and the shekel great,
    and deal deceitfully with false balances' (Amos 8.5),

thus condemning those who rig the measures and the currency, so that ordinary people have to pay too much money for too small quantities. Micah heard God say:

'Shall I acquit the man with wicked scales,
    and with a bag of deceitful weights?' (Micah 6. 11).

The importance of this is that it takes the authority of God out of the temple and the shrine and the church, out of the palace and the council chamber and the cabinet room, and brings it right into the shop and the factory and the supermarket. Just as there is nothing too great to be subject to the authority of God, there is nothing too small to be open to the interest of God. The authority of God is not something remote and distant; it is something by which every most ordinary action of every most ordinary life should be dominated and directed. It is then right to say that petty pilfering, shop-lifting, inefficient work, the taking of pay without giving value for wage, the offering of any service at an extortionate or dishonest price, the most massive robbery and the most petty dishonesty are all alike defiance of the authority of God. If we realise this, we then come to live in a world where there is no such thing as a little thing, for everything is done under God.

Cecil Pawson in his autobiography *Hand to the Plough* tells of the men who were the supreme influences on his life. One was Samuel Chadwick, and Pawson tells of

Chadwick's conversion. When Chadwick was ten, he heard a preacher tell at a Sunday School Anniversary that John Newton had once said that, if he were a shoe-black, he would be the best shiner of boots in the village. Cleaning boots was something that the young Chadwick knew all about. So Chadwick says: 'I hated to clean boots, especially father's Wellingtons. The Anniversary was a wet day, boot-cleaning next morning was at its worst. I began with the Wellingtons on the principle that the irksome part of a task is best tackled at once. I got through and put them down with a sense of relief. Then as I looked at them, the preacher's words about shining boots as if Jesus Christ was going to wear them chal-lenged me ... I wondered if these Wellingtons would look well on the feet of Jesus Christ. For answer, I took up the boots and began again. It was a simple thing to do, but I believe, in the light of after years, that it was the most important thing I ever did in my life. It was the adoption of a fixed principle from which I have never gone back. I got into the habit of doing the simplest duties as unto, and for, Jesus Christ.' That is the Chris-tian version of the Old Testament principle. The pro-phetic authority believed that even the commonest action was done in the sight of God.

viii. It is thus quite clear that for the prophet the authority of God permeates and pervades all life. The strange thing is what this all-pervasive authority did to life. It did not make life hard and stern and austere. It filled life with what one scholar called 'a high degree of sensitiveness', and 'a large-hearted benevolence'. It per-meated the whole community with the earthly reflection of the mercy of God. It was very often a compassion which was born from memory. 'You shall not pervert the justice due to the sojourner or to the fatherless, or take a widow's garment in pledge; but you shall remember that you were a slave in Egypt and the Lord your God redeemed you from there; therefore I command you to do this' (Deuteronomy 24. 17–18). It is as if to say: 'In your action to others remember what God has done for you. You went through it; remember others who are going through it.' So this authority of God demands a life which, as S. R. Driver says, is to be marked by humanity, philanthropy and benevolence, by equity and forbearance.

So the authority of God issues in a series of what have been well called the kindly laws of the Old Testament. If a man was passing through a vineyard or a field of standing corn, he might gather and eat grapes, or pluck and eat the heads of corn, always provided he did not gather the grapes into a container, or cut the corn with a sickle (Deúteronomy 23. 24, 25). The harvest was there to share, and not to hoard. When a man is harvesting his corn field, his olive grove, or his vineyard, he must not go back and gather a forgotten sheaf, he must not gather the last possible olive and the last possible grape; he must leave something for the stranger and the fatherless and the widow to glean. Once they were slaves themselves and they must remember what it is to be poor (Deuteronomy 24. 19–22). When a man is newly married, he must not be made to do military service or assigned a task which will take him from home. 'He shall be free at home one year, to be happy with his wife whom he has taken' (Deuteronomy 24. 5). The same is true of the man who has built a new house, or planted a new vineyard (Deuteronomy 20. 5–11). Sometimes when money is borrowed, a pledge has to be given. The mill at which the corn is ground, or even the upper mill-stone, must never be taken, for, if a man cannot grind his corn, he may starve (Deuteronomy 24. 6). The Jew wore a great seamless outer robe, which served him as a cloak by day and a blanket by night. If ever such a robe was accepted as a pledge, it must be given back at night for the borrower to sleep in (Deuter-

onomy 24. 12, 13). The hired servant must get his pay
before the day ends; the freed slave must not be sent
empty-handed to freedom; the escaped slave must not be
sent back to the slavery from which he has escaped (Deuteronomy 24. 14, 15; 15. 13, 14; 23. 15, 16). A blind man
must never be misled, and a deaf man must never be
cursed (Deuteronomy 27. 18; Leviticus 19. 14).

Even the animals are cared for. The nestlings may be
taken from a nest, but never the mother-bird (Deuteronomy 22. 6, 7). Corn was threshed by oxen drawing great
wooden sledges over it, and the ox must not be muzzled,
he must be free to eat (Deuteronomy 25. 4). Incidentally,
Paul for all his wisdom got this text wrong! He is arguing that the man who preaches the gospel has a right to
be supported by the gospel, and he quotes this text about
not muzzling the ox which is threshing. Then he asks: 'Is
it for oxen that God is concerned? Does he not speak
entirely for our sake?' (I Corinthians 9. 8–10). But indeed
it was for oxen that God was concerned, for the authority
of God legislates even for the beasts. A lost or a fallen
animal must not be left to its fate; it must be helped to
find its home or stand on its feet again (Deuteronomy 22.
1–4).

Even the sanitary arrangements of a camp are laid
down, a matter not without its importance in days when
there was no running water and no flushing toilets (Deuteronomy 23. 12–14). If in a war trees are to be cut down,
the trees to be cut are those which cannot be used for
food. 'Are the trees in the field men that they should be
besieged by you?' says the law quaintly (Deuteronomy 20.
19, 20). Even if there are favourites in a family, as is almost inevitable, the favouritism must not be allowed to
affect the allocation of the estate; favourite or not, a child
must have his rights (Deuteronomy 21. 15–17). A man
must always, in whatever he does, have a sense of responsibility for others. 'When you build a new house, you

shall make a parapet for your roof, that you may not bring the guilt of blood upon your house. if any one fall from it' (Deuteronomy 22. 8) – a doubly necessary rule, when the flat roof was the place of rest and prayer and meditation.

So in the life which the authority of God would have men live, there is this all-pervading kindliness and thoughtfulness, and the God who formed the earth and shaped the heavens and counts the number of the stars is the same God who cares that sanitary arrangements are made and kept and a house safely designed.

ix. One last thing remains to be said; in the conviction of the prophets the authority of God is an eschatological authority. That is to say, the effects and the consequences of it will be effective not only in this world, but also when this world is ended, not only in this life, but also when this life comes to an end, not only in time, but also when time is ended. Authority needs a sanction. If authority is to be real and effective, there must necessarily be consequences, if it is disobeyed, disregarded or defied. Authority, so to speak, must have teeth. The teaching of the prophets is that all things are moving towards the day of the Lord. At the day of the Lord this world, as it stands, will be disintegrated, there will be chaos, destruc- tion and above all judgment before the new age begins. The day of the Lord provides some of the most vivid and terrifying passages in the Old Testament. Zephaniah writes:

'The great day of the Lord is near,
     near and hastening fast;
the sound of the day of the Lord is bitter,
     the mighty man cries aloud there,
A day of wrath is that day,
     a day of distress and anguish,
a day of ruin and devastation,

a day of darkness and gloom,
a day of clouds and thick darkness,
    a day of trumpet blast and battle cry
against the fortified cities
    and against the lofty battlements.

I will bring distress on men,
    so that they shall walk like the blind,
    because they have sinned against the Lord;
their blood shall be poured out like dust,
    and their flesh like dung.
Neither their silver nor their gold
    shall be able to deliver them
    on the day of the wrath of the Lord.
In the fire of his jealous wrath,
    all the earth shall be consumed;
for a full, yea, sudden end
    he will make of all the inhabitants of the earth'
                                (Zephaniah 1. 14–18).

Isaiah writes:

'Behold, the day of wrath comes,
    cruel, with wrath, and fierce anger,
to make the earth a desolation
    and to destroy its sinners from it' (Isaiah 13. 9).

Joel writes:

'Alas for the day!
For the day of the Lord is near,
    and as destruction from the Almighty it comes'
                                (Joel 1. 15).

As the prophets saw time, the world was moving
towards the day of the Lord, and the day of the Lord
involved the annihilation of those who rejected the
authority of the Lord. To reject the authority of the Lord

was to court disaster on earth and destruction in eternity. Accept, they said, or be blasted out of existence.

So, in a word, the prophetic conception is of an authority of God which permeates and pervades life and every relationship in life with the awareness of God.

Chapter 2

Authority in the Old Testament
The Authority of Tradition

In the Old Testament the prophet stands for the authority of the Spirit. But in Judaism there were two other great figures, the priest and the Rabbi, and they embody the authority of tradition.

Before we can understand the place of the priest in the religious life of Judaism we have to have a clear idea of the conception of the *covenant.* The word covenant is a word for which no other word can be a substitute. If we were asked to suggest another word for covenant, we might suggest the words bargain, treaty, agreement, arrangement. But none of these words will do. In all these words there is the implication of two people coming together on equal terms to discuss the terms and the conditions on which they will embark on friendship and cooperation with one another. All these words imply the discussion between equals. But in the Bible the basic fact about the word covenant is that the whole initiative and the whole power is with God. It is not that man and God discuss things together and come to an agreement. In the covenant it is God alone who initiates the process; it is God alone who gives; and man can only take or refuse to take.

This is to be seen in the Greek word which the Bible uses for *covenant,* the word *diathēkē.* The usual Greek word for covenant is *sunthēkē. Sun* means *together,* and *thēkē* is from the verb *tithēmi,* which means *to place.* A

sunthēkē is therefore a placing of people together, a bringing of people into relationship, and the implication is
that the people involved enter into that relationship on
equal terms. But the biblical word for covenant, *diathēkē*, is the normal Greek word for a *will*, and a will is
the one kind of relationship between two people in
which the one party gives and in which the other party
can only take.

So in the covenant God on his own initiative, spon-
taneously, of his own will and of his own gracious choice
approached Israel with the offer that he would be their
God and that they would be his people. There is no discussion between God and Israel; there is no agreement
about terms and conditions. God offers; Israel takes.

But in point of fact the covenant did have its conditions; conditions laid down entirely by God and accepted
by Israel. In the first covenant Moses told the people all
the words and the ordinances of God. He sprinkled blood
on the people. 'Then he took the book of the covenant,
and read it in the hearing of the people; and they said,
"All that the Lord has spoken we will do, and we will be
obedient"' (Exodus 24. 1–8). This is to say that the covenant, the relationship between God and Israel was con-
ditional upon Israel accepting and obeying the Law.

The introduction of the Law into the matter at once
introduces an element of impossibility, for no man and
no nation can perfectly keep the Law. It is to meet that
situation that the priesthood and the whole sacrificial system was given. Sacrifice was the method by which
breaches of the Law could be atoned for and by which
the covenant relationship between God and his people
could be restored and maintained.

Clearly, this puts the priest in a position of immense
importance. Only the priest can offer sacrifice. The priest
has the exclusive right of sacrifice. Therefore, only
through the priest can every member of the community
fulfil his religious obligations, and only through the

priest can the covenant be maintained. There is introduced a tradition in which the authority of the priest is
supreme. Let us then look at the priest and the priesthood.

To begin with, the only qualification for the priesthood was birth. A priest must be a descendant of Aaron.
Pedigree was all-important. As far back as the days of
Ezra and Nehemiah certain priests were removed from
office because they could not produce their pedigree in
the genealogical registers (Ezra 2. 61–63; Nehemiah 7.
63–65). If a man was not a direct descendant of Aaron,
nothing could make him a priest. If he was a direct descendant of Aaron, nothing could stop him being a priest.
Character, education, ability did not enter into the matter. All that mattered was birth. In regard to marriage
the priesthood was equally exclusive. A priest could not
marry a harlot, a woman who had been defiled, or a
woman who had been divorced (Leviticus 21. 7). A priest
might not marry a woman who had been a prisoner of
war, because of the fact that she might have been violated. He might not marry a proselyte, nor the daughter
of a proselyte, nor an emancipated slave nor the daughter
of an emancipated slave. If the priest married the
daughter of another priest, he must enquire into her
pedigree for four generations back to make sure she was
of absolutely pure Jewish blood; if he married the
daughter of an ordinary Israelite, he must certify her
pedigree for five generations back.

The one thing which could and did preclude a man
from officiating as a priest was some physical blemish.
The original list of blemishes is listed in Leviticus 21.
16–23; he must not be blind or lame or have a mutilated
face or a limb too long; he must not have an injured foot
or hand; he must not be a hunch-back or a dwarf, or have
a defect in his eye-sight; he must not have an itching
disease or scabs or crushed testicles. Later the list of blemishes was extended to include one hundred and forty-two

different items. The descendant of Aaron so blemished could not officiate as a priest, but he was none the less entitled to share in all the many privileges and emoluments which fell to the priests.

There were obviously far too many priests for them all to serve at the one time in the Temple. So they were divided into twenty-four sections (1 Chronicles 24. 7–18). Even the sections were too big for all of their members to officiate at the one time, and so the different sections were divided into anything from five to nine subsections. Each of the sections was on duty twice a year for a week at a time. Only at the great festivals of Passover, Pentecost and Tabernacles were all on duty at the one time.

So we begin to see the privileged position of the priesthood, and the authority which in the very nature of things they exercised. They were clearly a highly exclusive body into which no outsider could possibly break, and their total working time could amount to no more than five weeks in the whole year.

In the second place, not only could only the priests offer the necessary sacrifices, but they could offer them only in Jerusalem. There had been a time when every town and village had its shrine; but these local shrines had been highly infected with the old Canaanite Baal worship. So one of Josiah's sweeping reforms was to abolish all the local shrines, and to centralise the whole of worship in the Temple at Jerusalem (2 Kings 23. 8). This clearly added to the monopolistic place of the priesthood. They were not only a highly exclusive body; their operations were concentrated in the one place. They possessed the keys of the gateway to the presence of God. They alone could carry out the rites and ceremonies which would restore the relationship with God, when it had been interrupted and broken by sin.

In the third place, the priests had perquisites such as can have fallen to few men in any society. It is a mistake to think that the sacrificial animals were commonly

burned entire on the altar. With the exception of the
burnt-offering, usually only a token part of the victim
was burned on the altar, and of the remainder the worshipper received some of the meat to hold a sacrificial
meal, and of all animals sacrificed the priests received a
share. It will be simplest if we set down the summary of
the privileges of the priests, as it is in Numbers 18. 8–19,
and then explain more fully what the various items involved.

> Then the Lord said to Aaron, 'And behold, I have
> given you whatever is kept of the offerings made to me,
> all the consecrated things of the people of Israel; I have
> given them to you as a portion, and to your sons as a
> perpetual due. This shall be yours of the most holy
> things, reserved from the fire; every offering of theirs,
> every cereal offering of theirs and every sin offering of
> theirs and every guilt offering of theirs, which they
> render to me, shall be most holy to you and to your
> sons. In a most holy place shall you eat of it; every male
> shall eat of it; it is holy to you. This also is yours, the
> offering of their gift, all the wave offerings of the
> people of Israel; I have given them to you and to your
> sons and daughters with you, as a perpetual due; every-
> one who is clean in your house may eat of it. All the
> best of the oil, and all the best of the wine and the
> grain, the first-fruits of what they give to the Lord, I
> give to you. The first ripe fruits of all that is in their
> land, which they bring to the Lord, shall be yours;
> everyone who is clean in your house may eat of it.
> Every devoted thing in Israel shall be yours. Every-
> thing that opens the womb of all flesh, whether man or
> beast, which they offer to the Lord, shall be yours;
> nevertheless the firstborn of man you shall redeem, and
> the firstling of unclean beasts you shall redeem. And
> their redemption price (at a month old you shall re-
> deem them) you shall fix at five shekels in silver, ac-

cording to the shekel of the sanctuary, which is twenty gerahs. But the firstling of a cow, or the firstling of a sheep, or the firstling of a goat, you shall not redeem; they are holy. You shall sprinkle their blood upon the altar, and shall burn their fat as an offering by fire, a pleasing odour to the Lord; but their flesh shall be yours, as the breast that is waved and the right thigh are yours. All the holy offerings which the people of Israel present to the Lord I give to you, and to your sons and daughters with you, as a perpetual due; it is a covenant of salt for ever before the Lord for you and for your offspring with you.'

Now let us see what this meant in practice. In the case of the sin-offering, which was an offering for man as a sinner, and the guilt or trespass offering, which was the offering for some particular sin, only the fat was burned on the altar and all the flesh went to the priests (Leviticus 6. 26; 7. 6, 7; Ezekiel 44. 29). In the case of the cereal offering, the offering of fine flour, wine and oil, only a handful was flung on the altar and all the rest belonged to the priests; and it is to be remembered that the cereal offering was never offered alone, but was offered along with every sacrifice that was offered (Leviticus 7. 9, 10, 14; 10. 12, 13; Ezekiel 44. 29). In the case of the peace offering, only the fat and the two kidneys were burnt on the altar; all the rest belonged to the priests (Leviticus 3. 1–17). The twelve loaves of the shewbread were replaced fresh every week, and the old loaves went to the priests (Leviticus 24. 5–9). The meat from these offerings had to be consumed in the Temple by the priests of duty in the Temple. Even in the case of the burnt-offering, the one offering which was consumed entire in the fire of the altar, the priests got the skins, a valuable perquisite in view of the number of offerings which were made (Leviticus 7. 8). In the case of the thank offering, the offering which the worshipper made to show his gratitude for some special mercy of God, the priests got the breast and the right thigh. In this case the meat could be consumed anywhere, by the families of the priests and by the priests who were not on actual duty in the Temple (Leviticus 7. 30–34; 10. 14, 15).

But apart altogether from their share of the sacrifices the priests enjoyed even greater perquisites. To them there came the first-fruits (Exodus 23. 19; 34. 26; Numbers 18. 13; Nehemiah 10. 35). These first fruits were the first fruits of 'the seven kinds' – wheat, barley, the vine, the fig tree, pomegranates, olives and honey (Deuteronomy 8. 8). This was an offering symbolically made to God, although the priests had the use of it. But the *Terumah*, the offering of the choicest fruits was a definite contribution to the priests. The *Terumah* was the giving of the choicest fruits of all that grows in the ground and of every tree, the most important items being the corn, the wine and the oil (Numbers 18. 12). The *Terumah* was exclusively for the use of the priests. The next contribution was the tithe (Numbers 18. 21–32; Nehemiah 10. 38, 39). The tithe was one-tenth of 'everything that can be used as food, and is cultivated, and grows out of the earth'. This tithing was observed with meticulous scrupulousness by the strictly orthodox (Matthew 23. 23; Luke 11. 42). The tithe was originally for the support of the Levites, who had to give a tithe of their tithe to the priests. Next there was the *Challah*, the offering of kneaded dough (Numbers 15. 17–21; Ezekiel 44. 30). Of any dough that was made from flour made from wheat, barley, spelt, oats or rye, the private individual, when he baked, had to give the priests one-twenty-fourth part, and the professional baker one-forty-eighth part.

Not even yet is the tale of the perquisites and privileges of the priests ended. Every firstborn male creature, whether of cattle or of men, was sacred to God (Exodus 13. 11–16; 22. 29, 30; 34. 19, 20; Numbers 18. 15–18; Deuteronomy 15. 19–23; Nehemiah 10. 36). If the animal was

a 'clean' animal (oxen, sheep and goats were clean) and if
it was free from blemish, then such an animal was treated
as a sacrifice. The blood was sprinkled on the altar and
the fat was burned on the altar; but the flesh belonged to
the priests, and could be eaten not only by the priests
serving in the Temple, but by priests residing anywhere
and by their families. If the animal was blemished, then
it belonged to the priests and was treated as ordinary
food (Deuteronomy 15. 21–23). If the animal was 'unclean' (horses, asses, camels were 'unclean'), then it had to
be ransomed, bought back, for a sum of money which
went to the priests (Numbers 18. 15, 16; Leviticus 27. 27).
This simply meant in practice that the priests collected a
sum of money for the firstborn of every 'unclean' animal.
In regard to the firstborn of men, to male children, the
child, when one month old, had to be ransomed, bought
back, for the sum of five shekels (Numbers 18. 15, 16; 3.
44–51; Exodus 13. 13; 22. 29; 34. 20). It is easy to see what
a source of income in cash and in kind the ransom of the
firstborn was to the priests. Still further, the priests were
entitled to the shoulder, the two cheeks and the stomach
of all animals slaughtered for sacrifice (Deuteronomy 18.
3). Still further, at the time of sheepshearing, anyone who
according to Shammai had more than two sheep, and
according to Hillel more than five, must give five selas of
wool to the priests (Deuteronomy 18. 4).

Not even yet is the tale finished. In a consecration vow
or a votive offering it was possible to dedicate anything or
anyone to God. Such things or people could be ransomed
back at a price; there was a regular scale for such buying
back (Leviticus 27), and the money went to the priests.
There was the possibility of dedicating people and things
irretrievably to God – persons, cattle, lands – and in this
case such things became the property of the priests (Leviticus 27. 28; Numbers 18. 14; Ezekiel 44. 29). Finally. if
something had been stolen, and if for any reason it was
no longer possible to return it to its original owners, a

penalty had to be paid, and that penalty was paid to the priests (Numbers 5. 5–8).

So then the priests were an exclusive body; their work would occupy them for no more than five weeks in the year; they had a truly astonishing array of privileges and perquisites; and in the most unique way they stood between men and God. It was through their agency alone that breaches of the covenant could be atoned for; they could open or bar the way to God.

Clearly, they both claimed and exercised a unique authority. Their position gave them a certain political slant. The priests were almost completely Sadducees. The Sadducees were the wealthy aristocracy. The Sadducees were the collaborationists with the Roman government; they were prepared to collaborate with anyone rather than lose their privileges and their comfort. The last thing the priests and the Sadducees wanted was a Messiah. A Messiah would only have caused trouble in which they might well lose their place and their wealth and their privilege.

It is to all intents and purposes certain that it was the Sadducees who were behind the death of Jesus. A most significant thing about the death of Jesus is that Jesus was not brought to Pilate on the charge of which the Jewish Sanhedrin had found him guilty. The charge of the Sanhedrin was a charge of blasphemy (Matthew 26. 63–66; Mark 14. 61–64; Luke 22. 67–71). But that is not the charge on which he was brought before Pilate. That charge was: 'We found this man perverting our nation, and forbidding us to pay tribute to Caesar, and saying that he himself is Christ a king' (Luke 23. 2).

It is entirely probable that the Sadducees were behind this. They knew very well that Pilate would not listen to a charge of blasphemy. He would dismiss that as a Jewish religious quarrel which had nothing to do with him. So the Sadducees turned the charge into a political charge. To them Jesus was a menace because he might arouse that trouble in which the Romans would have to act, and in which their position would be jeopardised and possibly lost. Therefore he had to be eliminated. To preserve their privileges, to preserve their authority, the Sadducees and the priests would stop at nothing to remove Jesus from the scene.

The simple statistics of sacrifice show clearly the place and the perquisites of the priests in the religion of Judaism. Every morning and every evening a lamb was offered. At Passover time daily for seven days there were offered two young bullocks, one ram, seven lambs, one he-goat together with the cereal and drink offerings (Numbers 28. 16–25). At the Festival of Pentecost the same was offered for one day (Numbers 28. 26–31). At the Festival of Tabernacles there were offered on the first day thirteen young bullocks, two rams, fourteen lambs, a he-goat and the usual drink and cereal offerings. On the six succeeding days the same offerings were made, except that one fewer bullock was offered each day (Numbers 29. 12–34). W. D. Davies in his book *Paul and Rabbinic Judaism* quotes an estimate of the sacrifices made in one year – 1093 lambs, 113 bulls, 37 rams, 32 goats, 5487 litres of fine flour, 2076 litres each of corn and wine. No one could live in Jerusalem without being aware of the sacrificial system.

It is a very dangerous thing for men to have such power and such privileges as the priests possessed. The Latin word for priest is *pontifex*, which literally means a *bridge-builder*. A priest is designed to be a bridge-builder between God and man, but he can make the toll price of his bridge into a barrier and not an approach. A priesthood can become a religious tyranny. Further, to surround men with privileges such as the priests possessed is to cushion them into a way of life which they will be very unwilling ever to let go.

The works of the prophets contain a terrific indictment of the false prophets and the priests. Malachi draws a

picture of what the priest ought to be, what he was meant
to be, and contrasts it with the picture of what he in fact
is: 'True instruction was in his mouth, and no wrong was
found in his lips. He walked with me in peace and uprightness, and he turned many from iniquity. For the lips
of a priest should guard knowledge, and men should seek
instruction from his mouth, for he is the messenger of the
Lord of hosts. But you have turned aside from the way;
you have caused many to stumble by your instruction;
you have corrupted the covenant of Levi, says the Lord of
hosts, and so I make you despised and abased before all
the people, inasmuch as you have not kept my ways but
have shown partiality in your instruction' (Malachi 2.
6–9). There stands the ideal and there stands the actuality.

The priest is accused of drunkenness. 'They also reel
with wine and stagger with strong drink; the priest and
the prophet reel with strong drink, they are confused
with wine, they stagger with strong drink; they err in
vision, they stumble in giving judgment. For all tables
are full of vomit, no place is without filthiness' (Isaiah 28.
7. 8). There is no one more scathing about the priests
than Jeremiah, himself of a priestly family. They are indifferent to God. 'The priests did not say, "Where is the
Lord?"' They are false. 'An appalling and horrible thing
has happened in the land: the prophets prophesy falsely,
and the priests rule at their direction' (Jeremiah 5. 30,
31). They are greedy for gain. 'From the least to the greatest of them, everyone is greedy for unjust gain; and from
prophet to priest everyone deals falsely' (Jeremiah 6. 13).
Even in the far back days of Samuel the priests were so
greedy for their share of the sacrifice that they would
hardly allow the worshipper to make his sacrifice before
they were forcibly grabbing their share and more than
their share (1 Samuel 2. 12–17). They were ignorant.
'Both prophet and priest ply their trade throughout the
land, and have no knowledge' (Jeremiah 14. 18). They
are ungodly. 'Both prophet and priest are ungodly; even

in my house I have found their wickedness, says the Lord'
(Jeremiah 23. 11). They are even murderers of the righteous. The sufferings of Jerusalem were 'for the sins of her
prophets and the iniquities of her priests, who shed in the
midst of her the blood of the righteous' (Lamentations 4.
13). Hosea is equally savage in his condemnation of the
priests. 'Hear this, O priests! Give heed, O house of
Israel! Hearken, O house of the king! For the judgment
pertains to you; for you have been a snare at Mizpah, and
a net spread upon Tabor. And they have made deep the
pit of Shittim. But I will chastise all of them' (Hosea 5. 1,
2). Those who should have pointed the way to God and
made it easier for others to walk were no better than a
snare for those who tried to walk in it. They are no better
than brigands and murderers. 'As robbers that lie in wait
for a man, so the priests are banded together; they murder on the way to Shechem, yea, they commit villainy'
(Hosea 6. 9). As Micah sees them, both priests and prophets are mercenary creatures. He says of Zion: 'Its heads
give judgment for a bribe, its priests teach for hire, its
prophets divine for money' (Micah 3. 11). Zephaniah says
of the prophets and priests: 'Her prophets are wanton,
faithless men; her priests profane what is sacred, and do
violence to the law' (Zephaniah 3. 4). The very men who
should be the guardians and protectors of what is sacred
are the destroyers of all that is holy. Malachi says of the
priests: 'A son honours his father and a servant his
master. If then I am a father, where is my honour? And if
I am a master, where is my fear? says the Lord of hosts to
you, O priests, who despise my name' (Malachi 1. 6).
They have offered polluted food on the altar and blemished animals for sacrifice. They have treated with irreverence the God whom it is their function to reverence.

We have here an example of an authority heir to, and
based on, a great tradition, exercising the very greatest
powers, and enjoying the greatest privileges, which yet
somehow went completely and selfishly wrong.

A religion which is based on sacrifice runs grave dangers. There is always the danger that a worshipper may come to think that, if he sins, all that he has to do is to offer the appropriate sacrifice and all will be well. Undoubtedly that was the popular view of sacrifice; sacrifice was regarded as an easy escape route from the consequences of sin. But it has to be remembered in fairness that that was very far from the ideal of sacrifice in Jewish religion. Three things have to be remembered when we enquire as to the real meaning of sacrifice in Judaism.

i. Sacrifice could only atone for sins unwittingly committed. In the instructions for sacrifice this is again and again stated (Leviticus 4. 2, 13, 22, 27; 5. 15–18; 22. 14). The word 'unwittingly' could be widely defined; it could be taken to mean not only sins committed in ignorance and unawareness, but sins committed, for example, in a moment of passion, when a man was swept into doing some wrong thing. Sacrifice did not and could not atone for sin committed with 'a high hand'. 'The person who does anything with a high hand, whether he is native or a sojourner, reviles the Lord, and that person shall be cut off from among his people' (Numbers 15. 30). The sin of the high hand is the 'presumptuous' sin (Numbers 14. 40–44; Deuteronomy 1. 43; 17. 12, 13). The meaning of this phrase 'with a high hand' can be well seen by comparing the translation of Exodus 14. 8 in the Authorised Version and in the Revised Standard Version. The passage is telling how the Israelites left Egypt. The A.V. has it: 'The children of Israel went out with a high hand.' The R.S.V. has it that Pharaoh pursued the people of Israel 'as they went forth defiantly'. The sin of a high hand is the defiant sin, the sin which knows well that it is deliberately disobeying God, the sin which takes its own way and knows that it is doing it. For that sin sacrifice brings no forgiveness.

ii. The second basic principle was that sacrifice without repentance was quite unavailing. 'There is nothing,' ran the saying, 'greater than repentance.' Repentance is the one thing God requires. Scripture was divided into three parts – the Law, which is the first five books of the Old Testament, the Prophets, and the Writings, which were the miscellaneous books remaining apart from the Law and the Prophets. So the Talmud has a passage: 'Wisdom (i.e. the Writings) was asked: "What is the penalty of a sinner?" and the answer was, "Evil pursues sinners" (Proverbs 13. 21). When Prophecy was asked the question it replied, "The soul that sins, it shall die" (Ezekiel 18. 4). When the Law was asked the question, it answered, "Let him bring a trespass-offering, and he will be forgiven"; as it is said, "And it shall be accepted of him to make atonement for him" (Leviticus 1. 4). When the question was asked of the Holy One, blessed be he, he replied, "Let him repent and he will be forgiven"; as it is written, "Good and upright is the Lord, therefore will he teach sinners in the way" (Psalm 25. 8).' The one essential for forgiveness is repentance. The teaching of Judaism is quite clear: 'Neither sin-offering nor trespass-offering nor death nor the Day of Atonement can bring expiation without repentance.'

There came the time after A.D. 70 when the Temple was destroyed and when Jerusalem was a heap of ruins, and when, therefore, sacrifice was impossible. Then it was said: 'Whence is it derived that if one repents, it is imputed to him as if he had gone up to Jerusalem, built the Temple, erected an altar and offered upon it all the sacrifices enumerated in the Law? From the text, "The sacrifices of God are a broken spirit"' (Psalm 51. 17). The sacrifice was only the outward and visible sign of the inward repentance. Without repentance the sacrifice was unavailing; with repentance no other sacrifice was necessary.

iii. The third basic principle is that the repentance must be real, and the only proof of the reality of repentance was that a man should change his ways. Johnstone

Jeffrey used to tell of the man who used to say: 'Life's just sinning and repenting, sinning and repenting, and it all depends on which you do last.' That is exactly the kind of repentance for which true Judaism had no use. The rabbinic teaching said: 'Whoever says, "I will sin and repent, and again sin and repent," will be denied the power of repenting.' The Talmud puts it this way: 'If a man is guilty of a transgression and makes confession of it, but does not amend his behaviour, to what is he like? To a man who holds a defiling reptile in his hand. Even if he immerse his body in all the waters of the world, his immersion is of no avail to him. But let him cast the reptile aside, and should he immerse in forty *seahs* of water (forty *seahs* was the irreducible minimum of water required for the bath to cleanse from ritual impurity), it immediately avails him; as it is said, "Whoever confesses his sins and *forsakes* them shall obtain mercy"' (Proverbs 28. 13).

In the highest form of Judaism sacrifice atoned only for unwitting sin; it was unavailing without repentance; and that repentance must be a true repentance which was not only sorry for its sins, but which also forsook its evil way. But inevitably the popular view was that sacrifice atoned for sin, as it were, automatically.

The priests exercised the authority of tradition, but it was an authority which in both priest and people had gone wrong.

There was in Judaism another form of traditional authority which was even more widespread and more universally effective than that of the priest. This was the authority of the Law. Law is rather an inadequate word for the basis of this authority. The word is *Torah*, which means *instruction* rather than law in the narrower sense of the term. The Torah was God's divine instruction on how to live.

The Jews were very specially and peculiarly the people of the Law – and strictly orthodox Jews still are. When the Jews under Ezra and Nehemiah returned from exile, they were faced with certain problems. Firstly, it was clear that they would have to abandon all hopes and dreams of political greatness. The population of Palestine was never more than four million, a number which compared with the great world empires was totally insignificant. Dreams of empire had to be laid aside, if the future was to be realistically faced. Secondly, the matter was even more serious. How is a nation so small to preserve its identity at all? A. Cohen in *Everyman's Talmud* quotes a saying of Zangwill; 'History, which is largely a record of the melting of minorities in majorities, records no instance of the survival of a group not segregated in space or not protected by a burning faith as by a frontier of fire.' The Jews made their choice. If they had to bid a long farewell to political greatness, then they would become as no nation had ever been or ever would be the people of God. That which would give them indestructible identity was and is the Law of God. So there came the day of decision when Ezra read the Law to the people and when they dedicated themselves to the acceptance of it (Nehemiah 8). So to them the Torah became everything.

'Great is the Torah,' ran the saying, 'which gives life to those who practise it in this world and in the world to come.' When a man studied the Torah, either alone or in company, the glory of God was with him. In the *Sayings of the Fathers* (6. 6) the necessities for the study of the Torah are listed.

The Torah is greater than the priesthood and than royalty, for royalty demands thirty qualifications, the priesthood twenty-four, while the Torah is acquired by forty-eight. They are: by audible study, distinct pronunciation, understanding and discernment of heart, awe, reverence, meekness, cheerfulness; by ministering to the Sages, attaching oneself to colleagues and discussion with disciples; by sedateness, knowledge of the Scripture and the Mishnah; by moderation in business, intercourse with the world, sleep, conversation, laughter, long-suffering, a good heart, faith in the wise, resignation under chastisement, recognising one's place, rejoicing in one's portion, putting a fence to one's words, and claiming no merit for oneself; by being beloved, by loving the All-present, loving mankind, loving just courses, rectitude and reproof; by keeping oneself far from honour, not boasting of one's learning, not delighting in giving decisions; by bearing the yoke with one's fellow, judging him favourably, and leading him to truth and peace; by being composed in one's study; by asking and answering, hearing and adding thereto (by one's own reflection); by learning with the object of teaching, and by learning with the object of practising; by making one's master wiser, fixing attention upon his discourse, and reporting a thing in the name of him who said it.

The Torah is altogether good. The Talmud has it:

What is the meaning of that which is written, 'Whoso keepeth the fig-tree shall eat thereof?' (Proverbs 27. 18). Why is the Torah compared to a fig? In all fruits there is a part which is refuse. In dates there are stones, in grapes there are pips, in pomegranates there are husks; but the whole of the fig is eatable. Similarly, in the words of the Torah there is no refuse.

It was a first principle that every word and every syllable of the Torah was meaningful, and that there was not a superfluous letter in it. This intense respect for the Torah produced four things.

i. It produced a system of schooling in which religious education was the only education, and in which the only textbook and lesson book was the Law. It was claimed that children began learning the Law with their swaddling clothes, that thus the precepts of the Law were graven on their souls, and that a child would sooner forget his own name than he would forget the instruction of the Law.

ii. It produced a race of teachers and interpreters. These were the Rabbis. The Rabbis were a curious mixture. No Rabbi might take any pay at all for teaching. It therefore followed that every Rabbi had to have a trade or a profession, by which he lived, while he gave his teaching free. The rabbinic saying had it: 'An excellent thing is the study of the Torah combined with some worldly occupation, for the labour demanded by them both makes sin to be forgotten. All study of the Torah without work must in the end be futile and become the cause of sin.' It was forbidden to make profit by the teaching of the Torah. 'Make not the Torah a crown wherewith to aggrandise yourself, nor a spade wherewith to dig. So also Hillel used to say: "He who makes a worldly use of the crown of the Torah shall waste away." Hence you may infer that whoever derives profit for himself from the words of the Torah is helping in his own destruction.' The result of this was that the Rabbi was very much involved in ordinary life. He was not shut up in some academic ivory tower; he was no remote and detached scholar. He knew and shared the life and work of the people he taught. But at the same time it was characteristic of the Rabbis that they demanded a special honour and special place. The New Testament more than once tells how they demanded the top places at feasts, the best seats in the Synagogue, how in their flowing robes and with the marks and symbols of their religion, they liked to walk through the market-places amid the respectful greetings of the ordinary people (Matthew 23. 5–7; Mark 12. 38, 39; Luke 11. 43; 20. 46). The Rabbis taught that a man's duty to them took precedence over his duty to his parents. If, for instance, a man's father and a man's Rabbi were taken captive, then it was his duty to ransom the Rabbi first, and his father only after that. A man's father, they said, brought his son into the life of this present world; a Rabbi brought him into the life of the world to come. So the Rabbis were a strange mixture of identification with the ordinary people and demanding pride.

iii. It produced the Synagogue. It is extremely probable that the beginnings of the Synagogue are to be looked for during the Exile in Babylon. In Babylon sacrifice was impossible, for sacrifice could only be offered in the Temple in Jerusalem. But even in a foreign land the Jews could observe the Sabbath, and on the Sabbath could meet to pray and to study the word of God – which was precisely what the Synagogue was for.

There was no competition between Temple and Synagogue; they existed for quite different purposes. The Temple existed for sacrifice; the Synagogue existed for the study of the Law. The Synagogue was 'the house of instruction'. The Synagogues have been called 'the popular religious universities of their day'. The official of the Temple was the priest; the official of the Synagogue was the Rabbi. Great as the Temple was, unique as the Temple was, it was the Synagogue which was the real centre of the religious life of Judaism. This was so for a very simple reason. There was only one Temple, the Temple in Jerusalem, and there must have been many and many a Jew who had never seen the Temple and who never would see the Temple. But the official ideal regulation was that, wherever there were ten Jewish families, a Synagogue must be set up. So wherever there were Jews, throughout Palestine and among the Jews dispersed all over the world, there were Synagogues. Ancient numbers always tend to be highly exaggerated. One authority says that there were three hundred and ninety-four Synagogues in Jerusalem alone, while another puts the number at four hundred and eighty. There was no Jew throughout the world who did not know the Synagogue.

The Synagogue was the beating heart of Jewish religion, and week by week in the Synagogue, the Torah was expounded to the people.

iv. The most important consequence of the place given to the Torah was the building up of the Scribal or the Oral Law. In Judaism and in the Bible the word Law is used in three senses. First, it means the Ten Commandments, which are the Law *par excellence.* Second, it means the Pentateuch, the first five books of the Old Testament, Genesis, Exodus, Leviticus, Numbers, Deuteronomy. For the orthodox Jew these books are the very essence of Scripture, and the other books are no more than commentary on them. Third, it means the Scribal or Oral Law. What is the Scribal or Oral Law? It was a first principle that the Law is perfect and complete. It contains everything which a man needs to live a life which will please God, a life which will bring him happiness in this world and blessedness in the world to come. If the guidance that is required is not there explicitly, it is there implicitly. It can be extracted by study and deduction. The Law as it stands consists of great principles. Out of these principles the Scribes and Rabbis aimed to find a rule for every possible man in every possible situation in life. In other words, the great principles have to be broken down into innumerable rules and regulations. Or, to put it in still another way, the Law has to be turned into legalism.

All this material was known as the Oral Law, because for centuries it was never written down, but carried in the memory of the Rabbis. All this mass was finally systematised by Rabbi Judah the Patriarch round about A.D. 200 in what is known as the *Mishnah.* The *Mishnah* contains six sections, with a total of sixty-three tractates, and in Herbert Danby's English translation makes a book of eight hundred and seventy-six pages. Let us then see how the minds of the Rabbis worked. We shall look at this rabbinic regulating of life from three directions – from the observance of the Sabbath, from the idea of cleanness and uncleanness, and from how all this appeared to a modern Jewish boy brought up in an orthodox Jewish home.

First, then, let us look at the rabbinic Sabbath law. This is of special interest, because it was his alleged breaking of the Sabbath law that brought Jesus into his initial collision with the orthodox Jewish authorities (Mark 2. 23–3. 6; Matthew 12. 1–14; Luke 6. 1–11; 14. 1–6). The initial Sabbath law is very simple:

> Remember the Sabbath day, to keep it holy. Six days you shall labour, and do all your work; but the seventh day is a sabbath to the Lord your God; in it you shall not do any work, you, or your son, or your daughter, your manservant or your maidservant, or your cattle, or the sojourner who is within your gates; for in six days the Lord made heaven and earth, the sea, and all that is in them, and rested the seventh day; therefore the Lord blessed the Sabbath day and hallowed it (Exodus 20. 8–11).

Here is the great special principle. Because God rested on the seventh day after the labour of creation, the seventh day is to be a day of rest, a rest to be shared by the labouring men and women and even the beasts. But the experts in the Law were not satisfied with a wide principle like that. Things must be much more closely defined than that, for above all things the Oral Law has a passion for definition.

In the *Mishnah* the tractate *Shabbath* on the Sabbath has twenty-three chapters. Obviously, the first question is – what is work? Work is defined under thirty-nine different classifications, 'fathers of work':

> Sowing, ploughing, reaping, binding sheaves, threshing, winnowing, cleansing crops, grinding, sifting, kneading, baking, shearing wool, washing or beating or

dyeing it, spinning, weaving, making two loops, weaving two threads, separating two threads, tying a knot, loosening a knot, sewing two stitches, tearing in order to sew two stitches, hunting a gazelle, slaughtering or flaying or salting it or curing its skin, scraping it or cutting it up, writing two letters of the alphabet, erasing in order to write two letters, building, pulling down, putting out a fire, lighting a fire, striking with a hammer, and carrying anything from one place of residence to another.

Even the suggestion of doing the prohibited action counted as doing it. When, for instance, the disciples, plucked the heads of grain when they were passing through the cornfields on the sabbath day, and when they ate the grain (Mark 2. 23–28), they were guilty of reaping by the action of plucking the heads, of winnowing and threshing by separating the grain from the husk, and, when they ate it, they were guilty of eating food which had been prepared on the sabbath.

Let us see how far this passion for definition could go. Nothing could be carried from one place to another. In Jeremiah 17. 21–24 we read:

Thus says the Lord: Take heed for the sake of your lives, and do not bear a burden on the sabbath day or bring it in by the gates of Jerusalem. And do not carry a burden out of your houses on the sabbath or do any work, but keep the sabbath day holy, as I commanded your fathers.

So then the carrying of a burden is forbidden. The next question is quite inevitable – what is a burden? So a burden is defined again and again – straw equal to a cow's mouthful, pea-stalks equal to a camel's mouthful, ears of grain equal to a lamb's mouthful, grass equal to a kid's mouthful, a dried fig's bulk of foodstuff, wine enough to mix the cup, milk enough for a gulp, honey

enough to put on a sore, oil enough to anoint the smallest
member (which is further defined as the little toe of a one-
day-old child), rope enough to make a handle for a
basket, paper enough to write thereon a tax-collector's
label, vellum enough to write, 'Hear, O Israel', ink
enough to write two letters of the alphabet, bone enough
to make a spoon, a pebble big enough to throw at a bird.
So they argued as to whether or not a cripple might go
out with his wooden leg on the sabbath, whether an artificial tooth might be used, whether a woman might wear
an ornament or a braid of hair, if a man might pick up
his child on the sabbath, and did it make any difference
if the child had a stone in his hand.

As for healing, steps might be taken to keep a man
from getting worse but not to make him any better. A
man, for instance, with toothache might drink vinegar,
but might not draw it through his teeth for that might
ease the pain. There were evasions too. Two letters of the
alphabet might not be written, but if they were written
in a non-permanent fluid, such as fruit juice, or if they
were written so that both could not be read together, for
instance, on each side of a corner, that was no sin. Knots
might not normally be tied, but, if a knot could be tied
or untied with one hand, there was no sin. A woman
could tie up her girdle. A bucket therefore could not be
tied to a rope on the sabbath day, but it could be tied to
a girdle.

Such was the rabbinic ingenuity applied to the Oral
Law, and it is to be remembered that in time this Oral
Law acquired even more authority than the written Law,
and it was the observance of it that was counted true
religion, pleasing to God. This was an authority which
turned religion into the observance of countless legal
acts. We may think all this a fantastic travesty of true
religion, but two things are to be remembered. First, no
one would keep all these rules and regulations, unless he
was desperately in earnest. Second, it was precisely the

observance of these regulations which made and makes the Jew different, and enables him to preserve his identity.

Second, we look at the conception of uncleanness. Uncleanness was not a physical thing. It was a ritual state. The consequence of uncleanness was that it disqualified a man from the worship of God and from sacrifice, and since uncleanness was contagious and infectious it disqualified a man from the society of his fellowmen. In his article on uncleanness in Hastings' one volume *Dictionary of the Bible* A. W. F. Blunt distinguishes five different areas of uncleanness.

i. There was what might be called sexual impurity. Ordinary sexual intercourse rendered a person unclean in the ritual sense of the term. The person remained unclean until evening, and had to immerse in a purificatory bath (Leviticus 15. 18). Sexual abstinence was demanded at the giving of the Law (Exodus 19. 15), and in war (1 Samuel 21. 5). Childbirth rendered a woman unclean for seven days and for the next thirty-three days she could not enter a sanctuary or touch sacred things. In the case of the birth of a girl the period was twice as long (Leviticus 12).

ii. There was uncleanness connected with blood. A menstruating woman was unclean, and rendered unclean everything she touched and all who had contact with her (Leviticus 15. 19–24). All abnormal discharges rendered a person unclean (Leviticus 15. 2–15; 25–30).

iii. There was uncleanness connected with food. The list of unclean animals is in Leviticus 11 and Deuteronomy 14. 4–21. It is futile to try to see reason in many of the prohibitions. Animals which were useful, dangerous, strange, who had evil qualities which might be transferred to the eater, animals in any way connected with heathen worship or deities were unclean, animals which were repulsive or uncleanly in their habits were unclean. The uncleanness of the pig was a wise rule, for the pig is an unclean feeder and harbours the trichina and tape worm which can be passed on to the eater, although in modern conditions the danger is practically non-existent. The list of clean and unclean birds seems without rhyme or reason.

iv. There was the uncleanness connected with death. To touch a dead body rendered a person unclean (Leviticus 22. 4–6; Numbers 5. 2; 6. 6–8; 9. 6, 7, 10; 19. 11–13; Haggai 2. 13). This is an idea which Judaism shared with many ancient religions. Perhaps it was due to what has been called 'the intrinsic mysteriousness of death'; perhaps it has something to do with ancestor worship, or with the danger of the spirits that hover round a corpse, or with the idea of death as a mark of the divine displeasure. There was a curious rabbinic belief that even Jahweh himself was unclean after he had buried the dead body of Moses (Deuteronomy 34. 5, 6), and had to be purified by fire.

v. There was the uncleanness connected with leprosy. A leper did not need only to be cured; he needed to be cleansed (Leviticus 13).

Such then is the conception of uncleanness, and it can be seen that there is no question of morality or of spiritual quality or of ethical rightness and wrongness; the whole thing is ritual, taboo, from beginning to end.

One of the most extraordinary tractates in the *Mishnah* is the tractate *Kelim*, which deals with the uncleanness of different kinds of vessels. To the rabbinic Jew this was clearly a matter of the first importance, because the uncleanness can be transmitted by the use of the vessel. The regulations are astonishing. The whole extraordinary edifice is based on Numbers 19. 14, 15: 'This is the law when a man dies in a tent, everyone who comes into the tent and everyone who is in the tent, shall be unclean seven days. And every open vessel, which has no cover fastened upon it, is unclean.' For thirty chapters and

forty-six pages the tractate pursues its fantastic way. We
take certain specimens of its regulations.

Utensils made of wood, leather, bone, glass, earthen-
ware and alum crystal, if they are flat, are not susceptible
to uncleanness; but, if they are hollow they are, not because they themselves contract uncleanness, but because
the airspace inside them does. On the other hand vessels
made of metal contract uncleanness whether they are flat
or hollow. It therefore follows that the first class of utensils
can be unclean inside but not outside, while the second
class can contract uncleanness both inside and out.
When they are broken they no longer contract uncleanness. Here at once there emerges one of these cases where
the rabbinic passion for definition emerges. What does it
mean for the utensil to be broken? In the case of earthen-
ware utensils, if they are used for food, the break must be
big enough for an olive to fall through, if for liquid, the
break must be big enough for the liquid to run through.
If they are wooden, the break must be big enough for an
average-sized pomegranate to fall through. In the case,
for instance, of a gardener's basket, the hole must be big
enough for a bundle of vegetables to fall through.

We quote three of the more fantastic rulings. 'The
cover of wine-jars and olive-jars and of papyrus jars are
not susceptible to uncleanness, but, if they were adapted
for other use, they are susceptible. If the cover of a stew-
pan has a hole in it, or if it has a pointed top, it is not
susceptible to uncleanness; if there is no hole in it, or if it
has not a pointed top, it is susceptible, because the house-
wife drains the vegetables into it.' 'If a shovel has lost its
blade, it still remains susceptible to uncleanness because
it has become the like of a hammer. If a saw has lost one
tooth in every two, it becomes insusceptible; but if there
is left a length of one *sit* (four thumbs' breadth) of teeth
at any one place, it remains susceptible.' 'If a three-legged
table lost one of its legs, it becomes insusceptible to un-

cleanness; if it lost a second leg, it is still insusceptible; but if it lost the third, it again becomes susceptible to uncleanness, if a man has the intention to use it (as a flat board) in this condition.'

It was obviously impossible for any ordinary man to live an ordinary life, and to observe all the thousands of rules and regulations, although he might try to do so. The one class of people who did accept and keep the Oral Law was the Pharisees. The name Pharisee means the separated one, and they separated themselves from ordinary life to concentrate on keeping every detail of the Law. There were never more than six thousand of them, and they were regarded as the fine flower of Jewish piety.

Here then is an authority, an authority based on tradition, an authority which turned religion into legalism. This is the Law by which, Paul said, no one could possibly get into a right relationship with God (Romans 3. 20; Galatians 2. 16). The whole object of such a law as this was to gain merit in the sight of God by one's own personal efforts in keeping it, and the first essential to a right relationship with God is to realise that we possess no merit of our own, and can never gain any.

Lastly, we look at what this rabbinic authority seemed like to a Jewish boy in an orthodox Jewish home in England, towards the end of last century, for the rabbinic law is still binding on a strictly orthodox Jew. The story is told in Victor Gollancz's *My Dear Timothy*, which is described as 'an autobiographical letter to his grandson'. All bus or train or tram riding was forbidden on the sabbath. So when the sun set early and the dark came in the afternoon, the young Victor had to walk home from St. Paul's school, on a Friday evening, the long miles from Hammersmith Broadway to Maida Vale. On the sabbath and on the festivals the journey from Elgin Place to Bayswater Synagogue in Chichester Place had to be done on foot.

Another taboo was that neither fire nor any of its derivatives could be touched on the sabbath. A Gentile was brought in to stoke and light the fire, but the instruction to tend the fire had to be given *before* the sabbath began, and not on the sabbath. Fire included light, and Victor Gollancz says: 'I remember very well also sitting one cold winter night on the lavatory seat in pitch darkness, because I "wasn't allowed" to switch on the electric light.' The Law forbids writing, painting, playing the piano, using a saw (for instance, for fretwork) or a hammer on the sabbath. Victor Gollancz as a boy liked painting. 'I can see a picture of myself now,' he says, 'as I write half a century later, up in our old nursery, with its bogus mahogany table, one afternoon ·in December. On the mantelpiece, above a roaring fire, were my colours and a brush and a cupful of water; and I was standing with a watch in my hand, waiting for the exact second at which, on the authority of the *Jewish Chronicle*, sabbath would that day "go out" and at last I could paint. The exact second was everything; the previous second you *couldn't*, the following second you *could*.' And Victor Gollancz points out that such was the authority of this tradition that even if no one knew that he had switched on the light or begun painting too soon, he just could not do it.

Victor Gollancz speaks about the edifice built on the thrice repeated injunction in the Old Testament: 'You shall not boil a kid in its mother's milk' (Exodus 23. 19; 34. 26; Deuteronomy 14. 21). The why and wherefore of this regulation are quite uncertain. Just possibly it is simply a prohibition of an action which infringes a decent reverence even for animal life. More likely, it may refer to a heathen custom of making such a broth and pouring it on the ground to increase fertility by magical methods. For the modern Jew this has no longer anything to do with boiling a kid in its mother's milk. It has become a reason for the most elaborate precautions to ensure that nothing derived from meat should ever come

into any kind of contact with anything derived from
milk. No kind of meat must ever be cooked with milk or
any of milk's products. Two sets of cooking utensils were
kept, one for cooking meat and another for cooking
which involved milk, two sets of plates, two sets of knives,
forks, spoons. If by some Gentile maid's mistake the utensils got mixed up, the plate was smashed, the pot or the
pan underwent elaborate purification. A meat knife
which had been used to cut butter or cheese had to be
buried in the earth before it could be used again. This
may look like a very primitive practice using Mother
Earth as a purifier. But Victor Gollancz writes: ' "With
my own eyes" I saw my mother doing it in an English
garden at the beginning of the twentieth century; and I
would have you know that my mother was a cultivated
lady, who had once had a piano lesson from Vladimir
Pachmann, and "read" at the Reading Room of the Brit-
ish Museum, and wrote plays.' To continue the deduc-
tions from the Old Testament prohibition, an orthodox
Jew would not dream of eating bread and butter with a
slice of meat. To eat butter with meat, for instance, with
steak, would be the final abomination. There must be an
interval between the eating of things connected with
milk and the eating of meat. For instance, after a meat
course at a meal the sweet course cannot contain milk or
cream or anything made of them, and cheese cannot be
eaten. Victor Gollancz says of his boyhood days: 'You
had to wait quite a time – interminably as it seemed to
my impatience – before eating a penn'orth of milk choco-
late after lunching on beef.' So on a simple and rather
obscure Old Testament prohibition a whole edifice of
eating ritual has been erected.

There were things connected with the Day of Atonement which even to a boy seemed strange and inexplic-
able. There was the twenty-four-hour fast during it, a fast
so absolute and severe that 'we were forbidden by our
parents to clean our teeth, lest a drop of water might be

swallowed'. So seriously was this taken that, 'We knew instinctively that to eat or drink on the Day of Atonement would be to do something monstrous and unnatural, something impossibly opposed to the order of things.'

There were things about the famous Day of Atonement Synagogue prayer which were puzzling. The prayer is the *Al 'Hit* ('For the sin'), a kind of comprehensive general confession. It consists of forty-four versicles each beginning with the words *Al 'Hit*, and each confessing its own sin, the sins being arranged alphabetically, two to each letter. The prayer is used several times throughout the day. It is said in a perfervid sing-song with the cantor leading, and is accompanied by forty-four beatings of the breast.

In the first place, the young Victor complained to his parents that he had never committed a sin before God 'by the taking of bribes', or 'in business', or 'by usury or interest', or 'by wanton looks'. It was explained to him that it did not mean him personally, or anyone else personally, but that in the prayer he was identifying himself with the whole Jewish people – and such a loss and surrender of individual identity seemed to him neither right nor desirable nor even real.

In the next place, his father was meticulous in his recitation of the *Al 'Hit*, and yet his father had a favourite phrase: 'I've never done anything wrong in my life.' It simply did not add up that a man might one day proclaim himself spotless and the next day confess to being guilty of every sin under the sun, beating his breast. Where was the reality in this?

For still another thing, the prayer prayed for forgiveness,

And also for the sins for which we owe a burnt-offering;
And for the sins for which we owe a sin-offering;

And for the sins for which we owe an offering, varying
according to our means:

And for the sins for which we owe an offering, whether
for certain or for doubtful trespass;

And for the sins for which we are liable to the penalty
of chastisement;

And for the sins for which we are liable to the penalty
of forty stripes;

And for the sins for which we are liable to the penalty
of death by the hand of heaven;

And for the sins for which we are liable to the penalty
of excision and childlessness:

For all these, O God of forgiveness, forgive us,
pardon us, grant us remission:

And also for the sins for which we are liable to any of
the four death penalties inflicted by the court – stoning,
beheading, burning and strangling.

The whole thing was unreal and yet it was intoned earnestly and even by some passionately, and by all as a
sacred duty.

And for one last thing – in some ways the most serious
of all. The congregation prayed for forgiveness:

'For the sin we have committed before thee by usury
and interest.' Victor Gollancz knew quite well there were
money-lenders in the congregation. 'These people were
money-lenders; they knew that they were money-lenders;
they publicly proclaimed that it was wicked to be a
money-lender; yet did nothing about it.' (An outsider
may interject that the defence would certainly have been
that it is sin for a Jew to lend at interest to another Jew,
but not to a Gentile.) But the young Victor had come to
the conclusion that 'a man's personal life was one thing
and the *Al 'Hit* quite another'. In other words, here was a
tradition which had all the authority in the world, and
which had not an atom of reality as the boy saw it.

So then in the Old Testament there was an authority of tradition. It was to be found among the priests, of whom on the whole it was true to say that generations of power and privilege had corrupted authority; and it was to be found in the Rabbi, in whom for many authority had become legalism, and tradition had become the meaningless binding upon people of laws and rituals and even prayers which had lost their reality.

Chapter 3

The Authority of Jesus

We remember the impression that a person has made on us long after we have forgotten the detail or even the substance of what he has said. A speaker will leave on us an impression of sincerity or insincerity. A teacher will leave us with the impression that he is a master of his subject or that he does not know what he is talking about. A person to whom we go for advice will leave us with the impression of decisiveness or of dither. We get the impression that one person will cope with anything that may emerge, and that another will prove a broken reed. W. E. Henley wrote many of his poems in hospital. He has one entitled 'The Chief', and in it there are the lines:

> His wise, rare smile is sweet with certainties,
> And seems in all his patients to compel
> Such love and faith as failure cannot quell.

He left the impression of one to whom it was not difficult to entrust one's life.

There is no doubt of the impression that Jesus left on those who listened to him. 'When Jesus finished these sayings, the crowds were astonished at his teaching, for he taught them as one who had *authority*, and not as their scribes' (Matthew 7. 28, 29). He had on him an air and atmosphere of authority.

The word in Greek is *exousia*, and it is a word which will repay study. It is a wide-ranging word.

i. It means place, or prestige or rank. Paul spoke of 'the governing authorities' (Romans 13. 1). The Book of Wisdom tells how in all his trials Wisdom preserved Joseph, till in the end she brought him 'authority over his masters' (Wisdom of Solomon 10. 14). *Exousia* brings power over other people.

ii. It frequently means the permission, or the right, or the opportunity to do something. Ecclesiasticus bids us to keep far from the man who has the *power* to kill, if we want to avoid the worry of the fear of death (Ecclesiasticus 9. 13). Plato has it that the constitution of Athens offers the *opportunity* to any Athenian who is not pleased with life at Athens to take his goods and go (Plato, *Crito* 51 D). He talks of the ennobling and the inspiring power of love, and he says: 'The law leaves a man *a free hand* for performing such admirable acts as may win praise' (Plato, *Symposium* 182 E). He says with penetrating truth that it is 'deserving of no slight praise, when a man with *a perfectly free hand* for injustice lives always a just life' (Plato, *Gorgias* 526 A). Xenophon depicts Socrates as condemning those who desire to bear the rule in cities that 'they may have *power* to embezzle, to treat others with violence, to live in luxury' (Xenophon, *Memorabilia* 2. 6, 24). The advice of Ecclesiasticus on bringing up a son is: 'Give him no authority in his youth' (Ecclesiasticus 30. 11). Do not give him the opportunity to do as he likes. If a person has *exousia* he is able to choose his own course of action.

iii. *Exousia* gives the power of control over people and circumstances. It is God alone who has fixed the times and seasons by his own *authority* (Acts 1. 7). '*The government* of the earth is in the hands of God' (Ecclesiasticus 10. 4). It is God alone who has *power* over life and death (Wisdom of Solomon 16. 13). No man has *authority* over the day of death (Ecclesiastes 8. 8). The sun has to have *authority* over the day, and the moon and stars over the night (Psalm 136. 8, 9). It is the Sage's advice: 'To son or

wife, to brother or friend, do not give *power* over yourself, as long as you live' (Ecclesiasticus 33. 19). *Exousia*
gives to a person the ability and the right to control. God,
for instance, has granted men *authority* over the things
upon the earth (Ecclesiasticus 17. 2). God gives man control over the world in which he lives.

iv. *Exousia* belongs to the person who has a certain
qualification or who holds a certain position. Thucydides
uses *exousia* in the sense of qualification to enter the
national games (Thucydides 5. 50). Aristotle speaks of
those who hold *higher positions* (Aristotle, *Rhetoric* 2. 6,
9). Aristotle says that the majority of mankind are content to live a life fit for cattle, but what can be expected,
when many persons of *high position* share the feelings of
Sardanapallus, which were summed up in the principle:
'Eat, drink and play, for all else is not worth the snap of
the fingers' (Aristotle, *Nicomachean Ethics* 1. 5, 3). To be
in *exousia* is to have the qualifications for entry to something worthwhile, or to be in a position which stands
above that of the common man. *Exousia* is a word which
very commonly goes with the description of official office.
It was usual to speak of the consular *exousia*, the consular
office or rank, or the *exousia* of the quaestorship, the office
of quaestor (Diodorus Siculus 14. 113; 8. 77). To have
exousia is to be someone special.

v. *Exousia* describes abundance of means or of power.
Thucydides said of the expedition against Sicily that it
was so lavishly equipped 'that it seemed more like a display of *wealth and power* to impress the rest of the
Greeks than an undertaking against enemies' (Thucydides 6. 31, 4). In a speech made by the Spartans Thucydides makes the speaker say that a people should not
change their customs because they now have a slight
superiority in *wealth and power*. 'It is not right that attributes which have been won through poverty should be
lost through prosperity' (Thucydides 1. 123, 4). To have

exousia is to have abundance of resources to deploy in the face of any situation.

vi. For this very reason *exousia* in secular Greek develops a bad meaning. *Exousia*, the power, the rank, the place, the prestige, the abundance a man possesses may produce in him a certain arrogance which is connected with *hubris*, the pride which despises man and defies God. As a halfway house to this meaning we may note that *exousia* in literary criticism is used for poetic licence. Julian writes in one of his orations: 'The poets have *unlimited licence* to invent' (Julian, *Orations* 1. 10b). Thucydides speaks of the *insolence* and the *arrogance* (*hubris* and *exousia*) of wealth (Thucydides 1. 38, 5). He speaks of the *insolence* and the *pride* of affluence which make men greedy (Thucydides 3. 45, 5). Demosthenes speaks of the intolerable impertinence of the man he is accusing: 'And then the *assurance* of the man!' (*De Falsa Legatione* 200). In the same speech (272) he warns against 'mockery, impunity, dishonour, unless you restrain the *licence* of these men'. *Exousia* can issue in an overbearing arrogance, and that is what the Jewish leaders were suggesting about Jesus, when they demanded: 'By what *authority* are you doing these things, and who gave you this *authority*?' (Matthew 21. 23).

After this survey of the general use of the word *exousia*, we may now look at the biblical use and especially its use in the New Testament. The word is used of every kind of authority.

(a) It is used of *royal* authority. Hezekiah showed to the envoys of Merodach-baladan all his possessions and all his *realm* (2 Kings 20. 13; Isaiah 39. 2). It is said by the Psalmist of God that 'Judah became his sanctuary and Israel his *dominion*' (Psalm 114. 2). Wisdom says to the Sage: 'In Jerusalem was my *dominion*' (Ecclesiasticus 24. 11). Antiochus, when disaster struck him, said in bewilderment: 'I was kind and beloved in my *power*' (1 Maccabees 6. 11). *Exousia* is regal authority.

(b) It is used of *domestic* authority. The man in the parable who went on a journey put his servants *in charge* (Mark 13. 34), that is to say, he left the control of the domestic arrangements in their hands. *Exousia* includes control of the family and the home.

(c) It is used of *legal* authority. Paul had *authority* from the chief priests to bind the Christians (Acts 9. 14; 26. 10, 12). The Jews watched Jesus closely to see if they could find a charge on which they could deliver him up to the *authority* and jurisdiction of the governor (Luke 20. 20). *Exousia* is the power of the law.

(d) It is used of *civil* authority. Every person is to be subject to the governing *authorities*, remembering that there is no *authority* except from God (Romans 13. 1–3). The faithful servant is given *authority* over ten cities (Luke 19. 17). Amongst the Gentiles the rulers and the great men exercise *authority* (Matthew 20. 25; Mark 10. 42; Luke 22. 25). *Exousia* is the authority by which the good order of the community and the state is established and maintained.

(e) It is used of *ecclesiastical* authority. Within the Church Paul has authority to build up and to destroy (2 Corinthians 10. 8; 13. 10), and if necessary, he will use it. *Exousia* is the power to exercise discipline within the fellowship of the Church.

(f) It is used of *military* authority. The centurion who appealed for the help of Jesus to heal his servant describes himself as a man under *authority* (Matthew 8. 9; Luke 7. 8). *Exousia* is the right to issue commands which dare not be disobeyed.

(g) In the case of Jesus *exousia* is used of *eschatological* authority. That is to say, the authority of Jesus extends beyond this life into the life to come. Jesus has the authority to convey to men forgiveness for sins (Mark 2. 10; Matthew 9. 6; Luke 5. 24). All *power* is given to him in heaven and in earth so that he is with his own to the end of time and beyond (Matthew 28. 18, 19). There are no limits to the authority of Jesus.

We began by saying that *exousia* is a wide-ranging word, and we have seen that indeed it is. Royal power, domestic power, legal power, civil power, ecclesiastical power, military power, eschatological power – all these are in the word *exousia* – and Jesus had *exousia*.

We shall very soon look in detail at the way in which Jesus expresses his authority; but before we come to the detail, let us look at three great areas of the work of Jesus in which the accent and atmosphere of authority are evident.

i. Jesus shows his authority in his *teaching*. We have already noted the reaction of those who heard him. 'And when Jesus finished these sayings, the crowds were astonished at his teaching, for he taught them as one having authority, and not as their scribes' (Matthew 7. 28). That reaction was there from the very beginning. On his first visit to the Synagogue at Capernaum the reaction was exactly the same (Mark 1. 21, 22).

This authority of Jesus was personal, for the thing which amazed his opponents was that, on their standards, he was an uneducated man. 'The Jews marvelled at it, saying, "How is it that this man has learning, when he has never studied?" ' (John 7. 15). And yet in spite of the fact that he had no technical theological education, his teaching was such that it struck the note of complete authority. Jesus was never afraid to use the word 'I' – to this we shall return. No scribe ever made a statement on his own responsibility. He always quoted this, that and the next rabbi. If Jesus quoted at all, he quoted scripture; but when he spoke, he spoke on his own authority or, to be more accurate, with the authority of God. As John makes him say: 'My teaching is not mine, but his who sent me' (John 7. 16). Jesus spoke as one who had the right to speak.

ii. Jesus shows his authority in his *healing*. Whatever argument there may be about the miracles of Jesus, there is no doubt that Jesus very successfully practised exorcism. And his exorcism was done with a word. 'What is this?' said the people in astonishment. 'A new teaching! With authority he commands even the unclean spirits, and they obey him' (Mark 1. 27). The Jews had their exorcists, but their methods were very different. Josephus tells us how the Jewish exorcists went about their business. The power to cast out demons had been part of the wisdom of Solomon, so Josephus writes: 'God also enabled Solomon to learn that skill which expels demons, which is a science useful and health-bringing to men. He composed such incantations also, by which distempers are alleviated. And he left behind him also the way in which to use exorcisms, by which they drive away demons so that they never return, and this method of cure is very effective to this day. I have seen a certain man of my own country, whose name was Eleazar, releasing people who were possessed by demons in the presence of Vespasian, and his sons, and his captains, and the whole multitude of his soldiers. The manner of the cure was this. He put a ring that had a root, which was one of those sorts mentioned by Solomon, in the nostrils of the demoniac, after which he drew out the demon through his nostrils. When the man immediately fell down, he adjured the demon never again to return into him, making still mention of Solomon, and reciting the incantations which he had composed. And when Eleazar would persuade and demonstrate to the spectators that he had such a power, he set a cup or basin of water some distance away, and commanded the demon, as he went out of the man, to overturn it, and thereby to let the spectators know that he had left the man; and when this was done the skill and wisdom of Solomon were very manifestly shown.' The difference between that method of exorcism, and the

calm authoritative word of Jesus, with no magic para-
phernalia at all, is immense (Josephus, *Antiquities* 8. 2,
5).

Josephus has a further account of how Jewish exorcists
worked. A certain root was much used in exorcism and
Josephus tells about it: 'In the valley of Machaerus there
is a root called by the same name. Its colour is like to that
of a flame, and towards evening it sends out a kind of ray
like lightning. It is not easily taken by such as would do
so, but recedes from their hands, nor will it yield itself to
be taken quietly until either the urine of a woman, or her
menstrual blood, is poured upon it. Even then it is certain death to those who touch it, unless one takes and
hangs the root itself down from his hand, and so carries it
away. It may also be taken in another way without danger, which is this. They dig a trench all round about it,
till the hidden part of the root is very small. They then
tie a dog to it, and when the dog tries to follow the person who tied him up, the root is easily pulled up, but the
dog dies immediately, as if it were instead of the man
who wishes to take the plant away. After this no one need
be afraid to take it into his hands. Yet after all these
pains in getting it, it is only valuable on account of one
virtue which it possesses, that, if it be brought to sick
persons, it drives away those called demons' (Josephus,
The Jewish War 7. 6, 3).

The book of Tobit tells how Tobit wishes to marry a
beautiful maiden called Sara. She has a great dowry and
she herself is a good person. But she has been married to
seven different men, all of whom perished on their wedding night, because Sara was loved by a wicked demon
who would allow none to approach her. Very naturally
Tobit was afraid, but the angel tells him: 'On the night
when you come into the marriage chamber, you shall take
the live ashes of incense and lay upon them some of the
heart and liver of the fish so as to make it smoke. Then

the demon will smell it and flee away, and will never again return' (Tobit 6. 16, 17). And so it was.

Jesus' method of exorcism was so very different from these Jewish methods with their incantations and their spells and their magic roots. To people who were used to these witch-doctoring methods the calm, quiet authority of Jesus must have come as an astonishment. He spoke the word with authority, and the sufferer was healed.

iii. Jesus shows his authority by his *actions*. To this we shall return. At present we are going to illustrate this by reference to only one incident, the Triumphal Entry (Matthew 21. 1–11; Mark 11. 1–10; Luke 19. 28–40; John 12. 12–15). The Triumphal Entry took place at Passover time, and at that time the city of Jerusalem was packed with pilgrims. Josephus says that the number of pilgrims at the Passover of A.D. 65 was 3,000,000. He later tells how the governor of Syria, Cestius Gallus, wished to convince Nero of the problem of governing Jerusalem. He asked the High Priest if a count of the pilgrims who attended the Passover could be taken. The priests took a count of the lambs sacrificed in the Temple, for every Passover lamb had to be sacrificed in the Temple, and its blood poured out on the altar. The number of lambs offered was 256,500. At the Passover meal the regulation was that there had to be a minimum of ten people, which means that there would be more people there than ten times the number of lambs, and Josephus estimates the number at 2,700,200. Even allowing for the fact that ancient writers always tend to exaggerate numbers, Jerusalem at the Passover time must have been crowded to the limit and beyond. It was at that time that Jesus chose to enter the city. It was abundantly clear that the enemies of Jesus were both eager and able to destroy him, and to enter the city was to challenge and defy the national and religious leaders.

Any prudent person in the circumstances of Jesus would have tried to slip into the city unseen; the last thing he would have tried to do would have been to court publicity. But Jesus entered Jerusalem in a way that was designed to focus every eye upon him. He came in not as a hunted criminal, but as a king coming to his own.

Every part of the entry was linked with royalty. When the people spread their garments on the ground they did what was done when Jehu became king. 'Then in haste every man of them took his garment and put it under him on the bare steps, and they blew the trumpet and proclaimed, "Jehu is king." ' (2 Kings 9. 13). When Judas Maccabeus and his followers rescued Jerusalem from the occupation of Antiochus Epiphanes, who had so savagely polluted it, it is said that they came in 'bringing ivy-wreathed wands and beautiful branches and also fronds of palm', and offering hymns of thanksgiving to God (2 Maccabees 10. 7). When Simon Maccabeus in a later freedom battle cleared the invaders from the citadel of Jerusalem, the people entered 'with praise and palm branches' (1 Maccabees 13. 51). The palm branches were the sign of victory. So Jesus entered the city like a king in conquest.

Still further, to a western understanding it is misleading to think of Jesus entering Jerusalem riding on an ass. For us, the ass is the despised donkey, whose highest function would be to give seaside rides for children. In the east the ass was a large and handsome animal. The ass was the animal of kings, and the king only rode on horseback when he was going to war. Deborah's victory song speaks of those who ride on tawny asses, and sit on rich carpets (Judges 5. 10). We read of Jair the Gileadite, the judge of Israel, that he had thirty sons who rode on thirty asses (Judges 10. 4), and of Abdon another judge that he had forty sons and thirty grandsons, who rode on seventy asses (Judges 12. 13, 14). The ass was the animal for the king and the princeling. Jesus was enacting the Zechariah prophecy:

'Rejoice greatly, O daughter of Zion!
   Shout aloud, O daughter of Jerusalem!
Lo, your king comes to you;
   triumphant and victorious is he,
humble and riding on an ass,
   on a colt the foal of an ass' (Zechariah 9. 9).

True, Jesus came as the king of peace, but it was as a king he came.

The Triumphal Entry was a demonstration of the claim of Jesus to royal authority. He came into the city as a king coming into his own. The whole incident was an invitation to the people of Jerusalem in which Jesus said to them: 'I offer myself to you as king.'

Let us now look in detail at the things in the Gospel narrative which demonstrate the authority of Jesus.

i. The authority of Jesus is demonstrated by the way in which he spoke. In the English text of the Sermon on the Mount there are 110 verses, and in these 110 verses there are 64 imperatives or commands. Jesus spoke in imperatives. He assumed the right to tell men what to do and how to live. He did not make the half-apologetic qualifications which most people make. He did not say: 'I think that you ought to do such and such a thing,' 'Perhaps you would be better to do this,' 'If I might make a suggestion,' 'I think that you ought to act thus, but I could be wrong.' He spoke in unqualified imperatives. Jesus did not even say as the prophets said: 'Thus says the Lord.' In his own name and his own right he made his uncompromising demands. Jesus is not the kind of person with whom we talk things over, or discuss things, or with whom we try to arrive at a reasonable compromise. We cannot take our decisions in regard to the claims of Jesus, as it were, *ad avizandum*, for consideration and consultation. The first step in the Christian life is to accept Jesus as the final authority, for that is what by the very accent of his teaching he claims to be.

ii. The authority of Jesus is demonstrated by his attitude to the Jewish Law. To the Jew the Law was the most holy, the most sacred, the most unchanging and unchangeable thing in the world. In spite of that six times Jesus quoted the Law – 'You have heard that it was said' – and six times he goes on to say: 'But I say to you.' Whether it be taken that Jesus was abrogating the ancient law, or whether it be taken that he was reinterpreting it, he could not have said anything more shocking to the ears of a Jew. To a Jew it must have sounded like an attack on the very foundations of religion and life.

'The Law is Israel's beauty, its strength, its comfort and its adornment.' 'The Law is the life of the Israelites: the cause of their continuance in this world, and the cause of their eternal life in the world to come.' The Law, said the Rabbis, was brought into existence a thousand generations before the world was created, and God himself looked into the Law before he created the world. Man was created on the day before the sabbath that he might begin his existence with an act of sabbath observance. They said that, when Moses went up to heaven, he found God sitting and weaving crowns for the letters of the Law. The crowns are the little flourishes which in the scrolls of the Law form ornaments to some of the letters. 'God,' they said, 'is more lenient to idolatry, unchastity and murder than to contempt of the Law.'

It is not surprising in view of the place which the Jews gave to the Law, that they insisted on the unchanging and unchangeable character of the Law. Maimonides was one of the very great Jewish teachers. He lived from A.D. 1135 to 1204, but although he lived long after New Testament times, his teaching contains the unchanging essence of Judaism. He laid down the thirteen principles of faith, and the ninth of them is:

I firmly believe that this Law will not be changed, and that there will not be any other Law, given by the Creator, blessed be his name.

The saying in Deuteronomy about the commandment to worship only God is followed by the saying: 'It is not in heaven, that you should say, "Who will go up for us to heaven, and bring it to us, that we may hear it and do it?"' 'It is not in heaven' – this was taken to mean that there is, so to speak, no more of the Law in heaven, that it has come complete and there is no more to come. The revelation in the Law is final, and there is nothing to be added to it. The Law speaks of an *everlasting* statute (Leviticus 16. 34), a statute given to last for ever. More than once there occurs the phrase 'an ordinance *for ever*' (Exodus 12. 14, 17). The Law is to remain unchanged for ever. Does not the Law say: 'God is not a son of man that he should change his mind?' (Numbers 23. 19). Did not the prophet hear God say: 'I, the Lord, do not change?' (Malachi 3. 6). In the Talmud it is said: 'The reading from the Prophets and the Writings may at some future time be discontinued, but the readings of the Pentateuch will never be abolished.' 'The things that are revealed belong to us and to our children *for ever*, that we may do all the words of the Law' (Deuteronomy 29. 29).

It is then natural that the test of any prophet was whether or not his message was in harmony with the Pentateuch, and, if it was not, he was a false prophet, and deserving of death. It is therefore only to be expected that to add to or to subtract from the Law is expressly forbidden. 'Everything that I command you, you shall be careful to do; you shall not add to it or take from it' (Deuteronomy 12. 32; in the Hebrew 13. 1). 'You shall not add to the word which I command you nor take from it, that you may keep the commandments of the Lord your God which I command you' (Deuteronomy 4. 2). Maimonides writes: 'It has been distinctly stated in the

Torah that its precepts remain in force for ever without change, diminution or addition.' He then quotes the texts from the Law which we have already cited, and then goes on: 'If therefore any man, whether an Israelite or a non-Israelite, should rise, perform signs and miracles, and say that the Lord sent him to add one precept or to abolish one of the divine precepts, or to interpret a precept in a way different from what has been handed down to us from Moses, or assert that the precepts which were given to Israel had only a temporary force, and were not permanent laws: such a man is a false prophet, because he contradicts the prophecy of Moses. The mission of the prophets after Moses is to exhort the people to obey the Law of Moses, and not to make a new religion.' M. Friedlander in his book *The Jewish Religion*, from which we have drawn much of the foregoing material, writes: 'Persons who address us in the name of God as his messengers, and bid us turn away from any of the laws commanded in the Pentateuch, are in our eyes impostors, who, knowingly or unknowingly, give forth their own opinions as divine inspirations.'

In view of all this it can easily be seen with what a sense of shock the orthodox Jews must have heard Jesus restate and reinterpret the Law. Here indeed was a claim to authority which to the Scribes and Pharisees and orthodox teachers and believers was nothing short of blasphemous. Friedlander quotes a saying from the Talmud. It is really aimed at those who engage in abstruse speculations about God, and forget the practical things – 'Would that they had forgotten me, and kept my commandments!' A saying like that shows the place that the commandments of the Law had, and the daring of the man who set out to challenge them.

iii. The authority of Jesus was demonstrated in particular in regard to the Sabbath Law.

To the Jew the sabbath was the most precious of all institutions. The Talmud tells with what loving devotion two Rabbis greeted the coming of the sabbath. 'Rabbi Chanina used to don his best clothes and towards sunset on Friday evening he would exclaim: "Come, let us go forth to meet Queen Sabbath."' Rabbi Jannai also used to dress himself in the best clothes he had, and say, as it were, to the sabbath: 'Enter, O bride; enter O bride!'

The great characteristic of the sabbath was that it was a day of rest, for it commemorated God's resting after the toil of creation (Exodus 20. 11; Genesis 2. 1, 2). To that end all work was forbidden. Among the things which were forbidden was healing, except in cases in which there was danger to life. A woman, for instance, might be helped in child-birth; and it was always allowed to attend to diseases of the ear, the eye, the nose, the throat, for these diseases were regarded as specially dangerous. But even when attention could be given to any trouble, steps could be taken only to see that the sick person did not get worse, not to make him better. This principle was taken to extraordinary lengths. A plain bandage might be put upon a wound, but not a bandage with ointment. Plain wadding might be put into a sore ear, but not medicated wadding. A broken limb might be made as comfortable as possible, but it might not be set. A dislocated limb might be washed, but might not have cold water poured over it, for that would have been to cure it. If a man had toothache, he might drink vinegar or use it as a relish, but he might not draw it through his teeth, for that would have been to take steps to ease the pain. If a man had a pain in his body, he might rub it with oil, because oil was so used every day as part of the ordinary toilet, but he might not rub his body with wine or vinegar or rose-oil, for all these were definitely medicinal. An artificial emetic might not be used. There was a drink called purgative water. A person might drink it in order to quench his thirst, but he might not drink it on the sabbath as a purge. If a wall collapsed, and if it was possible that some one was under it, enough might be cleared to see if there was anyone under it, to see if he was dead or alive, and to see whether he was a Gentile or a Jew. If he was alive, he could be freed, if he was a Jew, but if he was dead, or if he was a Gentile, he must be left until the sabbath had ended.

Jesus was well aware of these rules and regulations, and yet he repeatedly healed people on the sabbath day. He healed the man with the paralysed hand (Matthew 12. 9–14; Mark 3. 1–6; Luke 6. 6–11); the deformed woman (Luke 13. 10–17); the man with dropsy (Luke 14. 1–6); the man at the pool of Bethzatha (John 5. 2–16); the man born blind (John 9). For Jesus the test was human need. And if legalism stood in the way of human need, then he assumed the authority to break the Law and to help the need.

iv. The authority of Jesus was demonstrated in his approach to men. Jesus assumed an astonishing right to direct the lives of others. He came to Peter and Andrew, to John and to James, as they went about their tasks as fishermen, and said to them: 'Follow me' – and they did (Mark 1. 16–20; Matthew 4. 18–22; Luke 5. 1–11). No doubt they had already listened to him and talked to him. And then he came to them with a demand that they should leave their homes, leave their parents and relations, leave their jobs and set out with him on his one-man crusade. He demanded that at his command they should uproot themselves, that they should abandon safety and security, that they should bid farewell to a normal life and existence, and come with him on an adventure the end of which no man could see.

All three Gospel writers tell of the call of the Twelve (Matthew 10. 1; Mark 3. 13; Luke 6. 13). Mark puts it specially vividly – 'He called to him those whom he desired.' He decided whom he wanted, and then issued an imperious summons to them, which he expected them to accept. There is something literally extraordinary about the self-assumed authority of a man who selected the people he wanted, and told them, to leave everything and come with him. He demanded that loyalty to him should surpass the dearest and the most intimate loyalties in life. He insisted that loyalty to him must come even before loyalty to parents. To love father or mother, or wife and children, or brothers and sisters more than him was to show oneself unworthy and unfit to be his disciple (Matthew 10. 34–39; Luke 14. 26, 27). Luke's version of this saying of Jesus is much more alarming than Matthew's. Matthew has: 'He who loves father or mother more than me is not worthy of me; and he who loves son or daughter more than me is not worthy of me.' Luke has: 'If anyone comes to me and does not hate his own father and mother and wife and children and brothers and sisters, yes, and even his own life, he cannot be my disciple.' The two sayings are really the same. As E. F. F. Bishop points out in *Jesus of Palestine*, the Semitic languages have no middle terms. The choice is absolute. 'The Semite and the Arab particularly has no word for "compromise" in his vocabulary.' The stress in Luke's saying is not on hating your own people; the stress is on the absolute, unqualified, unconditional claim of loyalty to Jesus.

Another apparently heartless saying of Jesus also has to be read against its Palestinian background. There was a man to whom Jesus said: 'Follow me.' 'Lord,' he said, 'let me first go and bury my father.' 'Leave the dead to bury their own dead,' Jesus answered, 'but, as for you, go and proclaim the kingdom of God' (Luke 9. 59, 60). The point of that saying is that the man's father was not dead. The man was saying: 'Wait until my father dies and then I'll follow you.' In Palestine people married early and there was no reason why a man of forty should not have a son of twenty. So really the man was trying to put off his decision to follow Jesus for another twenty or thirty years or more. In this case Jesus is saying: 'You must decide, and you must decide now – and my claim on you must come first.'

And Jesus left no doubt that following him would involve. 'He who does not take his cross and follow me is not worthy of me' (Matthew 10. 38, 39; 16. 24, 25; Mark 8. 34, 35; Luke 9. 23, 24; 17. 33). Jesus' demand was not only to abandon all earthly ties, but to set out on a road at the end of which there stood a cross.

Jesus must indeed have had a unique consciousness of authority to make such uncompromising demands on men, and to summon them to leave everything for a cross.

v. The authority of Jesus is demonstrated in his public actions. His public career opens with an astonishing statement. 'He went throughout all Galilee, preaching in their Synagogues' (Mark 1. 39; Matthew 4. 23; Luke 4. 44). What would we say to a young man with no technical qualifications whatever, and with no ministerial training, who deliberately set out on a tour in which he proposed to preach uninvited in every pulpit in the land? In this country he would be arrested if he tried it. True, the situation was different in Palestine. The Synagogue was a very democratic institution. It had a president or ruler, as the New Testament calls him, but his duties were purely administrative. The Synagogue had no professional preacher. It had no minister or priest as a modern congregation has. Anyone who had a message to give might give it, if the president of the Synagogue was assured that he was a fit and proper person to address the people. None the less for a village carpenter from Nazareth with no rabbinic training whatsoever to contemplate making a preaching tour of the country shows a consciousness of authority far out of the ordinary.

But Jesus did more than that. From the orthodox point of view the most shocking incident in the public career of Jesus was the incident known as the cleansing of the Temple (Matthew 21. 12, 13; Mark 11. 15–17; Luke 19. 45, 46; John 2. 13–16). In that incident Jesus drove from the Temple – John says that he even used a whip to do so – the changers of money and the sellers of sacrificial victims. Every year all Jews had to pay a Temple tax. That tax could only be paid in coins which had no king's head on them, because, if there was a head on the coin, the coin became a graven image. This tax had to be paid at Passover time, when people from all over the world gathered in Jerusalem. For ordinary purposes any kind of currency was valid. To pay the tax only shekels of the sanctuary and Galilean shekels were accepted. The money-changers in the Temple were there to change unacceptable into acceptable coins, which was indeed a public service; but they charged a rate, first, for changing the coins of the pilgrims, and, second, for giving them change, which meant that the poor pilgrims were being forced to pay fifty per cent more than they ought to. Most people who came to the Temple brought a sacrifice. Sacrificial victims could be bought outside the Temple, but a victim to be fit for a sacrifice must be without spot or blemish. The Temple authorities had appointed inspectors to examine the victims. If the victim had been bought outside the Temple, it was quite certain that the inspectors would find a blemish, and the pilgrim would be compelled to buy his offering at the official Temple shops where the victims had already been inspected. This again sounds like a public service, but there were occasions when a pair of pigeons would cost as little as five new pence outside the Temple and as much as seventy-five new pence inside the Temple.

Three things infuriated Jesus about this. First, the whole business was a ramp in which pilgrims were being ruthlessly fleeced. Jesus' action was first of all a blow for social justice. Second, the huckstering and the bargaining and the arguing must have made the place a pandemonium in which any kind of prayer or meditation or worship was quite impossible. Third, the whole business was taking place in the Court of the Gentiles, the only part of the Temple into which a Gentile might come. This meant that, in the one place where it was open to the Gentile to worship, worship was impossible. The action of Jesus was a blow for social justice, a scathing rebuke of irreverence, a defence of the rights of the Gentiles.

But think of it. This carpenter from Nazareth has taken upon himself to rebuke the religious leaders of the day. This outsider has taken upon himself to cleanse the Temple. And he speaks of it as 'his father's house'. He assumes the right to do what he likes with the Temple because it belongs to him. That was the most astonishing display of authority that Jesus ever enacted.

vi. The authority of Jesus is demonstrated in his personal claims.

It is demonstrated in his claim in regard to life. Jesus claimed to be the only safe foundation on which any man can build his life. He does this in the parable of the two builders, which both Matthew and Luke relate (Matthew 7. 24–27; Luke 6. 47–49). This parable tells how a wise builder took the trouble to dig down until he struck rock, and on that rock he built his house, and of a foolish builder who built on the sand. Then the tempest came, wind and storm and rain and floods, and the house of the wise builder stood fast, but the house of the foolish builder collapsed, and there was nothing but a heap of ruins. There are certain things to be said about this story.

First, it is the story of a practical man. Jesus had built houses and he knew what he was talking about. We underrate Jesus when we call him a carpenter. He was in Greek a *tektōn*. A *tektōn* was a craftsman. In every village there used to be a craftsman who, with the very minimum of tools, and with only his natural skill to help him would make you almost anything – a chair, a table, a coffin, a bridge, a house. Jesus was not a handless academic. He was talking out of firsthand knowledge.

Second, the story that Jesus told was the kind of thing that happened. In Palestine in summer many streams dried up completely. So a careless man, looking for a site

to build a house might find a sandy hollow and think
that he had found the very place he wanted. He might
then begin to build directly on to the surface of the sand
without excavating down to the rock. Then the winter
came, and the pleasant sandy hollow became the bed of a
rushing torrent, and the house was swept away by the
floods.

Third, not only did this kind of thing happen; it still
happens. Out of his long experience in Palestine Eric
F. F. Bishop in *Jesus of Palestine* cites modern examples
of it. He writes: 'When the C.M.S. hospital was being
built in Salt before the war on a site intended for many
years, the local church committee deplored the lack of
proper foundations, for there was not the needed digging
and deepening. They were right, for the foundations
were undermined by the rainfall on the hill behind, seep-
ing through and causing cracks on the important walls.
The result has not been as devastating as in the picture
presented by our Lord, but the repairs have cost more
than the hospital.' He tells of leaving Amman after the
morning service to return to Jerusalem in a deluge of
rain. When they came to the Wadi Shaib, which had
been dry in the morning, as it was for most of the year,
and which had no bridge over it, they found it a raging
torrent and had to wait for two hours before their car
could cross it. He tells of houses on the Gaza–Askelon
road swept completely away, because the wadi changed
its course. The floods come like a river, and are usually
preceded by a high wind the day before.

It is Jesus' claim that he is the only sure foundation for
life. Life founded on any other foundation will be swept
away by the storms of life.

There is an implicit claim to a quite unique authority
in the form of many statements put into the mouth of
Jesus in the Fourth Gospel. There are many who would
hold that the sayings put into the mouth of Jesus in the
Fourth Gospel were not actually spoken by him, but are

rather expressions of the faith which the Christian community had in Jesus, and affirmations of that which they had found him to be. Even if that is so, they are still evidence for our enquiry, for then they would become responses from men to the authority which emanated from Jesus. The sayings in question are the 'I am' sayings. 'I am' sayings are specially characteristic of Jesus, and specially characteristic of the Fourth Gospel, and they have very definite overtones.

There are times when 'I am' sayings are no more than colourless statements of fact. So, 'I am Joseph' (Genesis 45. 3); Peter's saying: 'I am the person for whom you are looking' (Acts 10. 21); Jesus' 'I am Jesus whom you are persecuting' (Acts 9. 5). These are no more than simple statemants of fact.

But in the Old Testament there is an 'I am' which has been described as 'the style of deity'. '*I am* your God' (Genesis 17. 1). '*I am* the Lord your God who heals you' (Exodus 15. 26). '*I am* your deliverance' (Psalm 35. 3). '*I am* the Lord who loves righteousness' (Isaiah 61. 8). '*I am* God, and also henceforth I am he' (Isaiah 43. 13). *I am* is a phrase which is often found in the sayings of God. In statements of special stress the 'I' is doubled. '*I, I am* he that comforts you' (Isaiah 51. 12). '*I, I am* he who blots out your transgressions' (Isaiah 43. 25). '*I, I am* the Lord, and besides me there is no saviour' (Isaiah 43. 11). This way of speaking goes back to Exodus 3. 14 where God's name is revealed as 'I am who I am', and where Moses is told to tell the people '*I am* has sent me to you'. This comes over into the New Testament in the Revelation. '*I am* alpha and omega' (Revelation 1. 8; 21. 6; 22. 13). '*I am* the first and the last' (Revelation 1. 17; 22. 13). In any Jewish saying 'I am' is characteristic of God. This 'I am' method of speaking is characteristic of Jesus in the Fourth Gospel.

I am the bread of life (John 6. 35).
I am the light of the world (John 8. 12).

I am the door of the sheep (John 10. 7, 9).

I am the good shepherd (John 10. 11).

I am the resurrection and the life (John 11. 25).

I am the way, the truth and the life (John 14. 6).

I am the real vine (John 15. 1).

All these 'I am' sayings are spoken 'in the style of divinity', with the accent of God. Jesus assumes the right to speak as God speaks, or, if we are to argue that the words represent the faith of the Church rather than the actual words of Jesus, the impression that his hearers had when they were listening to Jesus was that they were listening to God.

There is an even more striking use of 'I am'. It is used by Jesus – and this happens in the Synoptic Gospels as well as in the Fourth Gospel – without any predicate, simply 'I am' all by itself. It is used of Jesus at his trial. 'Are you the Christ, the Son of the Blessed?' the high priest asked him, and he answered: *'I am.'* In the Fourth Gospel in the conversation with the Samaritan woman, the woman says that when Messiah comes he will tell them everything. Jesus' answer is literally: *'I am*, he who is speaking to you' (John 4. 26). In the Greek there is no 'he'; it is simply *'I am'*. In John's account of the arrest of Jesus in the Garden, Jesus asks those who have come to arrest him: 'Whom do you seek?' They answered: 'Jesus of Nazareth.' Jesus said to them: *'I am.'* In the Greek there is no 'he'; it is quite simply *'I am'*. When the disciples saw Jesus walking on the water, and were terrified, Jesus said to them: 'Take heart, *I am*' (Mark 6. 49, 50; cp. Matthew 14. 27; John 6. 20). The English versions translate it: 'It is I.' And so it can be translated, but the Greek is exactly the same, *egō eimi*. 'I am'. So in John we find Jesus depicted as saying: 'Before Abraham was, *I am*' (John 8. 58). 'You will die in your sins, unless you believe that *I am*' (John 8. 24). Once again, there is no 'he' in the Greek, simply *'I am'*. Jesus said to them: 'When you have lifted up the Son of Man, then you will know that *I am*' (John 8. 28). Once again, in the Greek there is no 'he', simply '*I am*'.

In the Greek Old Testament this use of 'I am' with no predicate is only in the words of God. In the song of Moses there is the verse: 'See now that I, even I, am he, and there is no god beside me' (Deuteronomy 32. 39). In the Hebrew it is simply: 'See, see that *I am*'. 'You are my witnesses,' Isaiah hears God say, '... that you may know and believe that *I am* he' (Isaiah 43. 10). As usual, there is no 'he' in the Hebrew. 'Even to your old age *I am*' (Isaiah 46, 4).

The interesting thing is that, as Deissmann has shown in *Light from the Ancient East*, this 'I am' form of statement is just as much 'the style of deity' in religious writings of the Hellenistic religions as it is the Old and the New Testaments.

Deissmann quotes, for instance, an inscription in honour of Isis, whose worship was widespread in the ancient world in New Testament times: '*I am* Isis, the queen of every land, taught by Hermes, and whatsoever things I have ordained, no one is able to lose them. *I am* the eldest daughter of Cronos, the youngest god. *I am* wife and sister of King Osiris. *I am* the first that devised fruit for men. *I am* mother of Horus the King. *I am* she who rises in the dog-star. For me was the city of Bubastis built. Rejoice, rejoice, Egypt that nourished me.' The heathen goddess too uses the same 'style of deity', the 'I am'. Deissmann also quotes a magical document: '*I am* the headless demon, having eyes in my feet, the strong one, the deathless fire. *I am* the truth who hates the fact that evil deeds are in the world. *I am* he who lightens and thunders. *I am* he whose sweat is a shower falling upon the earth to make it fruitful. *I am* he whose mouth burns altogether. *I am* he who begets and begets again. *I am* the grace of the aeon.'

It is quite clear that in the Old Testament, in the New Testament, and in the pagan religious language, the 'I

am' is characteristic of the speech of God. Jesus' words
were the words of deity. There was nothing less than the
accent of divine authority on his lips.

Jesus did not only speak in 'the style of deity'; he
claimed to be to men the unique revelation of God. Later
in this chapter we shall be returning to this. At the mo·
ment we note only one supreme claim: 'No one comes to
the Father but by me' (John 14. 6). It is to be clearly
noted what Jesus is claiming when he said this. He did
not say that no one came to *God* except through him.
Paul was later to say that the created world produces such
evidences and signs of God that anyone who does not see
God in God's world is beyond excuse (Romans 1. 19, 20).
Many men had come to *God*. What Jesus opened the way
to was *God as Father*. It is not difficult to arrive at the
idea of a creating God. God, as a famous astronomer said,
must be a mathematician. And as Sir James Jeans said:
'No astronomer can be an atheist.' But when man is feeling like a lost child out in the rain, when life has fallen
in and the sun has set at midday, when we are prostrated
with sorrow or torn with bewilderment, a God who is a
mathematician is not much good to us. George Bernanos
said that throughout his whole life his inspiration was
'the God whom we have learned to know as a wonderful
living friend who suffers in our sorrow, rejoices in our
joy, who will share our death agony and receive us in his
arms, upon his heart'. That is why for Bernanos, as R. C.
Zaehner says in *Drugs, Mysticism and Makebelieve,* the
supreme and central things in Christianity were the
agony in the Garden and the cry of utter desolation on
the Cross. The plain fact is that without Jesus no man
would have known God the Father. It is true that no one
comes to *the Father* but through him – there lies his
authority.

vii. The authority of Jesus is demonstrated in his
claim that his effect on the lives of men is not confined to
this world, but is also exercised in the world to come. His

claim is that his authority does not end with this world. He claims the right to direct the lives of men in this world and to settle their destinies in the world to come. This side of Jesus confronts us with certain basic truths about the Christian life.

(a) In the first place, judgment is an essential part of Jesus' message. The word judgment is often on his lips (Matthew 5. 21, 22; 10. 15; 12. 36, 41, 42). Life – death – judgment is the process of the Christian life. Christianity is clear that life in this world is not a self-contained matter; it is the first chapter of a continued story; and the second part will be dependent on what happened in the first part. Jesus has no doubt that a man is on the way to judgment.

(b) Jesus was by no means afraid to use the word hell. There was a place where there would be wailing and gnashing of teeth (Matthew 13. 42, 50; 22. 13; 24. 51; 25. 30; Luke 13. 28). There was a place of punishment.

The Gospels use two words for hell. They use the word Hades (Matthew 11. 23; 16. 18; Luke 10. 15; 16. 23). Originally Hades was the place to which all the dead went, a grey, shadowy, strengthless, colourless realm, where men lived like shades and ghosts. This was before men had any real doctrine of a life to come at all. But by the time of the Gospels Hades, certainly in the parable of the rich man and Lazarus, has become a place of punishment (Luke 16. 23). The other word is Gehenna, the Greek form of Ge Hinnom, the valley of Hinnom. This had been the place where children were once sacrificed to Moloch the fire-god. Josiah had stopped the worship, and had made the valley an unclean place. In later days the valley of Hinnom became the refuse dump and public incinerator of Jerusalem with a thick pall of black smoke for ever brooding over it and a loathsome worm breeding amidst the refuse. So revolting a place it was that it became a symbol for the place where the wicked would be destroyed (2 Kings 23. 10; 2 Chronicles 28. 3; 33. 6;

Matthew 5. 22, 29; 10. 28; 18. 9; 23. 15, 33; Mark 9. 43, 45, 47; Luke 12. 5). Jesus did not contemplate a life in which at the end of the day it would be the same for everyone. There was judgment and there could be punishment to come.

(c) Equally Jesus spoke of the reward of eternal life (Matthew 19. 16; 25. 46; Mark 10. 17, 30; Luke 10. 25; 18. 18). And in the Fourth Gospel eternal life becomes Jesus' highest gift to men (John 3. 16; 6. 54, 58; 17. 2, 3). The word for *eternal* is *aiōnios*. *Aiōnios* does not describe something which simply lasts for ever; in *aiōnios* there is *quality* as well as *quantity* of life. The only person to whom the word *aiōnios* can properly be assigned is God. Eternal life is therefore the life of God. So the reward is nothing less than a share in the life of God.

(d) But now we come to the specially significant parts of the pattern. The right of judgment belongs to Jesus. Both the Synoptic Gospels and the Fourth Gospel are sure of this. It is the Son of Man who is going to sit on the throne at the final judgment (Matthew 25. 31). 'The Father judges no man, but has given all judgment to the Son' (John 5. 22). Jesus has authority as the Son of man to execute judgment (John 5. 27). Jesus is Saviour, but Jesus is also judge.

(e) The standard of judgment was two fold. A man would be judged on the grounds of the conformity or the non-conformity of his life to the kind of life Jesus commanded men to live. It is not the man who glibly says, 'Lord, Lord', who will be saved; it is the man who obeys the will of God (Matthew 7. 21–23). The man who will enter into life is the man who in this life has shown to men the loving care and concern which Jesus exemplified in himself and urged on others (Matthew 25. 31–46). The test will be whether or not a man's conduct is founded on the teaching and example of Jesus.

(f) Now we come to the supreme claim. The claim of Jesus is that in the last analysis a man's eternal destiny will be settled by the man's reaction to him. If a man confesses him before men, he will confess that man before God (Matthew 10. 32; Luke 12. 8). If a man believes in Jesus he is exempt from judgment; he already has eternal life; he has passed from death to life (John 5. 24). This is simply to say that, if a man accepts the claim of Jesus, then he is safe from judgment, and his eternal destiny is life. What eternity will be like depends on a man's reaction and attitude to Jesus. So Jesus claims the last and the final authority, the authority to settle the destiny of every man.

When we are confronted with someone who claims the right to dictate what kind of life we shall live in this life and to settle what kind of destiny we shall have in the next, our first reaction must be to demand what right this person has to speak like that. We are bound to ask the same question as the chief priests and the elders: 'By what authority are you doing these things, and who gave you this authority?' (Matthew 21. 23). In other words, we are compelled to ask the question which every age is compelled to ask: 'Who is this Jesus?'

It is my conviction that no one ever gave a better answer to the question, and no one ever will, than the John of the Fourth Gospel, when he said: 'The Word became flesh and dwelt among us' (John 1. 14). The Word – in Greek the *Logos*. This word Logos has two meanings; it means *word* and it means *reason*. There is no one English word which covers both meanings. Because of this Moffatt retains *Logos*, and has: 'The *Logos* became flesh', and leaves the expositor to explain. What is it then that this word *Logos* says about Jesus? There are three directions from which we may come at this, and each of them has something relevant to say.

i. We come at it from the quite general direction. In any language there are two things which can be said about a word. First, a word is a means of communication; it is by the use of words that people communicate with each other. *Jesus is God's means of communication.* Jesus is the living word through whom and by whom God enters into communication with men. Second, a word is the expression of a thought. I think, and then I look for words through which I can express my thought. *Jesus is the expression of the thought of God.* To call Jesus the *Logos* is to say: 'If you want to hear what God wants to say, look at Jesus. If you want to see how God thinks, look at Jesus.'

ii. We may come at it from the Jewish direction. In the Old Testament God's word is God's creating power. In the creation story, it is always: 'And God *said*...' (Genesis 1. 3, 6, 9, 14, 20, 24, 26). The Psalmist has it: 'By the word of the Lord the heavens were made' (Psalm 33. 6). God's word was God's creating power, and *Jesus is God's re-creating power.* God's word was the agent in the first creation. Jesus the Word is God's agent of creation in the new creation.

iii. We may come at this from. the Greek direction. *Logos* in Greek does not only mean word; it also means mind or reason. Heraclitus the ancient Greek philosopher six hundred years before Jesus came into the world, said: 'All things happen according to the *Logos*.' The Greeks were fascinated by the order of the world. Why is this a dependable universe? Why does the same effect always follow the same cause? Why is H_2O always water? Why if you plant turnip seeds, do you always get turnips? What solves the traffic problem of the heavens? What keeps the planets in their courses and never allows any of them, so to speak, to run amok? That, they said, is the work of the *Logos*, the work of the reason which is at the heart of the universe, and that reason is nothing other than the mind of God. The *Logos* is the mind of God, interpenetrating the universe, making sense of all things, and making man a reasonable creature. *So then Jesus is the mind of God.* 'The Word became flesh' – the mind of God became a human person. This is to say: 'If you want to see how God's mind works, look at Jesus.' Jesus is the embodied mind of God.

Herein we see the source of Jesus' authority, and herein we see who and what Jesus is. It is not right to say simply and without qualification that Jesus is God. There are attributes of God that we do not see in Jesus. Jesus, when he was in the flesh, was not omnipresent; he was able to be in only one place at one time. Jesus was not omniscient; there were things he did not know. For instance, he did not know the time and the hour of his coming again (Mark 13. 32). That, he said himself, was known only to God. Jesus was not omnipotent. There were places and circumstances in which he could do no mighty works (Mark 6. 5). In the human Jesus the great metaphysical attributes of God – omniscience, omnipotence, omnipresence – are not to be seen. In John's Gospel Jesus speaks no fewer than forty times of being sent into the world. In regard to God Jesus was under orders. All through his life Jesus prayed – and he cannot have been praying to himself. Jesus did not, as the Fourth Gospel has it, say: 'He who has seen me has seen *God*.' What he did say was: 'He who has seen me has seen the *Father*' (John 14. 9). This is to say that in Jesus we do not see the abstract God of the theologians and the philosophers; but we do see, perfectly and completely in full revelation, the Father, the attitude of God to men, *how God feels to me*. In Jesus there is full displayed the mind of God to men.

The authority with which Jesus spoke, his claim to direct life on earth and settle destiny in heaven, show that he was aware of this. And this means certain things.

Jesus' awareness of a special relationship to God must have been a growth and a development. The New Testament is not afraid of the idea of growth and development in Jesus. 'Jesus increased in wisdom and in stature, and in favour with God and man' (Luke 2. 52). It is clear that the baby Jesus at his mother's breast, the little child who needed all things done for him, could not possibly at, say, three months old have been filled with thoughts, or even aware, of a special relationship to God. Such an infant would have been a monster, not a human being.

This means that Jesus went through the same process as the prophets. He had an experience, and then through life he maintained the vision which the experience had given to him. His experience, I think, came to him in two parts. It came to him first when he was a boy in the Temple (Luke 2. 41–51). In that moment he had the sensation of being in his Father's house. For eighteen years that experience, which came to him when he was twelve, grew and deepened. More and more he became aware of his special, his unique relationship to God. But, I think, that at first and for a long time he was not aware that that experience had, as it were, anything to do with anyone else except himself. It was something private, personal, for him alone. Then there came the emergence of John the Baptist when Jesus was thirty, and Jesus was baptised (Luke 3. 23; Mark 1. 9–11; Matthew 3. 13–17; Luke 3. 21, 22). And in that second moment Jesus became aware that this special relationship with God was no personal and private thing; it had been given him to make him Messiah, Saviour of men. He discovered that his experience was not for his own sake, but for the sake of mankind. It meant that no longer could life be lived and God, so to speak, enjoyed in the quiet of Nazareth. He had to go out on the ways of men and he had to embark on the way of the Cross.

So then like all the prophets Jesus had his experience, and like all the prophets he then had to maintain the contact with God and the awareness of the call. This he did through prayer. Luke's Gospel is the Gospel of prayer. Luke consistently shows us Jesus at prayer. Jesus prayed before his baptism (Luke 3. 21). He went into the wilderness to pray in the solitude with God before his first open clash with the Pharisees and teachers of the

Law (Luke 5. 16). Before he chose the Twelve, he spent all night in prayer (Luke 6. 12). He prayed before he asked Peter the all-important question at Caesarea Philippi (Luke 9. 18). He had gone up the mountain to pray when the incident called the Transfiguration happened (Luke 9. 28). He was himself praying when his disciples came to him with the request to be taught how to pray (Luke 11. 1). His prayer in Gethsemane with the Cross looming ahead was an agony and a wrestling, not so much with God, as with himself, to ensure his obedience to the will of God (Luke 22. 41). He brought his life to an end on the Cross with a prayer, and the prayer he then prayed was the first good-night prayer that every Jewish mother taught her child to pray before the frightening dark came down (Luke 23. 46; Psalm 31. 5). And it is entirely significant that when Jesus took that prayer of the Psalmist and made it his own, he prefaced it with one word which the Psalmist did not use – the word *Father* – '*Father*, into your hands I commit my spirit.' It was an experience given by God, and fed with prayer, which gave Jesus his authority.

One point remains – if the experience of Jesus was a growing and developing awareness of God and of his own relationship to God, and if that awareness had to be, and was, maintained by the life-line of prayer, then that awareness was something which could have been lost. Goodness only becomes possible when a man could have taken the wrong way and took the right way. Temptation is not temptation, unless the person tempted has the real possibility of falling. A test is no test, if there is no possibility of failure. Unless in Gethsemane there was a real possibility that Jesus could have turned back, unless he could have refused the will of God, unless he could have evaded the Cross, then the agony of Gethsemane loses all its agony, and becomes unreal play-acting. The supreme greatness of Jesus was that the whole purpose and plan of God depended on him – and he did not fail.

The authority of Jesus was an authority to direct men's lives and to settle men's destinies, and it came to him, as it came to the prophets, with a vision of God, the force and vividness of which were maintained by prayer. The authority of Jesus was given and maintained by God.

Chapter 4

Authority in the Church
In the New Testament

Community means discipline, and discipline means
authority. Whenever any group of people agree to come
together, whether it is in a Church or in a golf club, there
have to be rules by which they live. That is, there must be
discipline. And equally there must be some means to deal
with the person who refuses to abide by the rules. That is,
there must be authority.

In the case of the early Church discipline and authority
were absolute necessities. The early Church, it has
been well said, was like a little island of Christianity in
the middle of a sea of paganism. The early Church was
open to the most dangerous infections. There was an
ethical threat and a theological threat.

The ethical threat was desperately real. Juvenal the
Roman satirist lived from about A.D. 60 to 120. In his day
he said: 'Vice is at its acme' (*Satire* 1. 149). 'No deity,' he
said, 'is held in such reverence among us as wealth' (*Satire*
1. 112, 113). The fever of gambling was such that men
came to the tables not with a purse but with a treasure-
chest, and with a cashier instead of an armour-bearer
(*Satire* 1. 86–93). It was an age in which, as Gibbon has
recorded, fourteen out of the first fifteen Roman Em-
perors were homosexuals. Marriage had to all intents and
purposes broken up. In Rome it was the regular custom
to identify the years by the names of the consuls in office.
But, Seneca says, women reckoned the years not by the

names of the consuls but by the names of their husbands, and for a woman to live without a paramour was not a proof that she was chaste, but simply a proof that she was ugly (Seneca, *On Benefits* 3. 16). To have a child was not a privilege but a disaster. Even the Empress Messalina found her pleasure in acting as a common prostitute; Claudius was Emperor and her husband. Juvenal writes of her: 'As soon as his wife perceived that her husband was asleep, this august harlot was shameless enough to prefer a common mat to the imperial couch. Assuming a night-cowl, and attended by a single maid, she issued forth; then having concealed her raven locks under a light-coloured peruque, she took her place in a brothel reeking with long-used coverlets. Entering an empty cell reserved for herself, she there took her stand, under the feigned name of Lycisca, her nipples bare and gilded, and exposed to view the womb that bore you, O nobly-born Britannicus! Here she graciously received all comers, asking from each his fee; and when at length the keeper dismissed his girls, she remained to the very last before closing her cell, and with passion still raging hot within her went sorrowfully away. Then exhausted by men but unsatisfied, with soiled cheeks, and begrimed with the smoke of the lamps, she took back to the imperial pillow all the odours of the stews' (*Satire* 6. 116–132). It is an astonishing picture of the woman who was Empress of the world and who chose to practise as a common prostitute. 'Will Hiberina be satisfied with one man?' asks Juvenal. 'Sooner compel her to be satisfied with one eye!' (*Satire* 6. 53, 54). When Paul wrote the first chapter of the Letter to the Romans he said no worse about Rome than the Roman moralists did themselves. Persius, Rome's other great satirist, lived from A.D. 34 to 62; he was an exact contemporary of Paul. He talks of 'filthy Natta, numbed with vice, whose heart is so over-laid with fat lard, that he has no sense of sin, no knowledge of what he is losing'. Persius prays to God that men 'may look upon virtue and pine that they have lost her for ever' (*Satire* 3. 31–38).

This is the kind of world in which the early Church was living, and the Church needed discipline exercised by authority to preserve its purity against the infection of the world.

Not only was the Church in ethical peril; it was in theological peril too. In Greek thought there had always been a suspicion of the body; there had always been the feeling that, if a man could only divest himself of the body and become pure spirit, his troubles would be at an end. There was the Orphic jingle, 'Sōma sēma', the body is a tomb. The thought is common in Philo, that learned Jew who tried to tie together Jewish religion and Greek thought. The chief cause of ignorance is the flesh and association with the flesh. Nothing presents such a hindrance to the growth of the soul as the flesh. 'It is not easy to believe in God because of the mortal companion with which we are yoked.' Plato spoke of the prison house of the body. Epictetus called himself a poor soul shackled to a corpse. Seneca spoke of the detestable habitation of the body. Deep in Greek thought there was embedded this hatred of the body.

In due time this worked itself out into a way of thought called Gnosticism. Gnosticism asked the age-old question: Whence sin and suffering and evil? It answered the question in this way. It held that from the beginning there were two realities – God and matter. God is pure spirit, and altogether good. Matter from the beginning is essentially flawed and essentially evil. The Christian doctrine of creation is creation out of nothing. But Aristotle had said: 'It is impossible for anything to be made out of that which is not.' So the Gnostics held that this world was created out of that original matter. And this means that from the beginning the world was

made out of bad stuff. Creation did not become bad; it is
originally bad. Creation is not reformable; it is essentially bad.

If matter is bad, it means that the God who is altogether good, the God who is pure spirit, could not himself touch it. He therefore put out a series of aeons or
emanations. Each aeon or emanation is a little further
from God, and a little more ignorant of God. At last the
series ends in an aeon or emanation who is distant from
God, and who is not only ignorant of God but who is also
hostile to God. And by that distant, ignorant, hostile
aeon or emanation, the Demiurge, this world was created.
Therefore the world and all that is in it is essentially bad.
This has the most dangerous consequences.

i. If matter is bad, then the body is bad. If the body is
bad, we can do either of two things with it. We can practise a rigid asceticism, refusing the body its every desire,
regarding every desire and instinct of the body – and
especially the sex instinct – as completely evil. Or, we can
argue that since the body is evil, it does not matter what
we do with it. Therefore sate and glut its desires. Give it
its way; since it is evil anyway, it makes no difference. In
either case Christian morality, the Christian ethic, is
wrecked.

ii. The same thought applies to the whole world. If
matter is evil, the whole world is evil. Earth is indeed a
desert, and there is neither light nor joy.

iii. If matter is evil, and if the body is evil, then there
is no possibility of an incarnation. God could never have
taken a human body. The Gnostics therefore regarded
Jesus as a phantom without a real body. He left no foot-
step on the ground when he walked. When you touched
him there was nothing there. He was never seen to eat
and his eyes were never seen to blink. The humanity of
Jesus was destroyed.

iv. The human spirit could escape, but it needed to
learn all the passwords which would take it past the vari-

ous aeons and emanations on the way up to God. Each aeon had its mythology; each aeon had its password; all this had to be learned, and only the intellectually able could learn it. And so real religion came to be beyond the reach of the ordinary man and became the privilege and the perquisite of the chosen few. The result was inevitably the idea of first and second-class Christians.

If Gnosticism had been allowed to continue unchecked Christian morality, Christian fellowship, and the very idea of the incarnation would have been destroyed. The Church needed discipline and authority to counter this.

The Gospels are clear that this authority of discipline was given to the apostles by Jesus. According to Matthew's Gospel Jesus said to Peter: 'I will give you the keys of the kingdom of heaven, and whatever you bind on earth shall be bound in heaven, and whatever you loose on earth shall be loosed in heaven' (Matthew 16. 19). 'Truly, I say to you, whatever you bind on earth shall be bound in heaven, and whatever you loose on earth shall be loosed in heaven' (Matthew 18. 18). 'Jesus breathed on them, and said to them, Receive the Holy Spirit. If you forgive the sins of any, they are forgiven; if you retain the sins of any, they are retained' (John 20. 22, 23). There are two pictures in these sayings. Binding and loosing were the regular rabbinic expressions for prohibiting and permitting, admitting and excluding. So the power is given to the apostles to make and to relax the principles and the rules of discipline, to admit to and to exclude from the fellowship. The picture of the keys comes from the saying about the appointing of Eliakim as steward in Isaiah 22. 20–22: Shebna is to be replaced by Eliakim as steward: 'In that day I will call my servant Eliakim the son of Hilkiah, and I will clothe him with your robe, and will bind your girdle on him, and will commit your authority to his hand; and he shall be a father to the inhabitants of Jerusalem and to the house of Judah. And I will place on his shoulder the key of the house of David; he shall open and none shall shut; and he shall shut, and none shall open.' The possession of the keys is the sign of stewardship. It is the sign of a delegated rather than of a personal authority. The steward is the keeper of the church on behalf of Jesus Christ.

It is true that the apostles were clad with a very special authority in the early Church, but it is also true that this in no way produced a hierarchical dictatorship. In the New Testament story the decisions are regularly taken by the body of the congregation. When an apostle had to be chosen to replace the traitor Judas, it is Peter who moves the motion, but it is the congregation who puts forward the candidates (Acts 1. 15–26). When men had to be chosen to see to the charitable work of the Church, once again it is the Twelve who make the suggestion, but it is the congregation who do the choosing (Acts 6. 1–6), and the apostles who do the approving and the setting apart. When Peter took the crucial step of admitting Cornelius the Gentile to the fellowship of the Church, it was to the congregation he had to explain himself and to justify his action (Acts 11. 1–4). When the Council of Jerusalem took the great decision to open the doors to the Gentiles, the decision was approved by the apostles and the elders with the whole Church (Acts 15. 22). When Paul called upon the Church at Corinth to take disciplinary action against the man guilty of notorious immorality, that action is to be taken 'when you are assembled', at a meeting of the congregation (1 Corinthians 5. 4). Leadership the apostles had, but in no sense did they have dictatorship. The decision was in the hands of the congregation.

The disciplinary action took different forms. It might consist of admonition, encouragement and rebuke: 'Admonish the idlers; encourage the faint-hearted; help the weak; be patient with them all' (1 Thessalonians 5. 14). It might take the place of first personal remonstrance, then remonstrance before witnesses, and finally citing before the congregation: 'If your brother sins against you, go and tell him his fault, between you and him alone. If he listens to you, you have gained your brother. But if he does not listen, take one or two others along with you, that every word may be confirmed by the evidence of two or three witnesses. If he refuses to listen to them, tell it to the Church' (Matthew 18. 15–17). If the wrong-doer consistently persists in his error, then the fellowship of the Christian congregation must be withdrawn from him. If he is impervious to personal appeal, to the presence of witnesses, and even to the Church, then he is to be treated as a Gentile and a tax-gatherer (Matthew 18. 17). The advice in regard to those who create dissensions and difficulties is: 'Avoid them' (Romans 16. 17). Within the Church the Christian must not associate with immoral men (1 Corinthians 5. 9). To such a man the name of brother cannot be given (1 Corinthians 5. 11). A factious man is to be admonished once or twice; after that 'have nothing more to do with him' (Titus 3. 10).

The Jew knew about what could be called excommunication, expulsion from the Synagogue. Anyone who accepted Jesus as the Messiah was to be put out of the Synagogue (John 9. 22). In Paul's letters we twice come upon a terrifying phrase. The Corinthians are urged to deliver to Satan the notoriously immoral man (1 Corinthians 5. 5). Paul says that he has delivered Hymenaeus and Alexander to Satan that they may learn not to blaspheme (1 Timothy 1. 20).

This phrase has a double background. It has a Jewish background. It was very probably used when a man was cast out of the Synagogue, when he was excommunicated. In that usage it stems from God's words to Satan about Job. God is giving Satan permission to submit Job to any test, and, as the Greek literally has it in the Septuagint, God says to Satan: 'Behold, I am handing him over to you. Just this one thing – spare his life' (Job 2. 6). So the man ejected from the Synagogue was handed over to Satan. But the phrase has also a Greek background. The

Greeks had a custom of execration in which they devoted a person who had wronged or injured them to the gods of the underworld, by means of a prayer to these gods and by the use of a cursing tablet. The tablet was thrown into the earth, usually into a grave, and was thus supposed to find its way to the underworld. The technical word was to deliver such a person to these gods. So the formula is: 'Demon of the dead, ... I deliver unto you N.N., in order that...' So both Jews and Greeks were familiar with the idea of delivering some one to Satan.

It is important to see what the phrase implies. It was not, at least in Jewish custom, the destruction of the man that was desired. In the Job passage it is a condition that Job's life was to be spared. In the Corinthians passage (1 Corinthians 5. 5) it is Paul's hope that, even if the man's flesh is destroyed, his spirit may be saved. And in the Timothy passage (1 Timothy 1. 20), it is apparently the hope that Hymenaeus and Alexander will learn to stop blaspheming. Paul's statement to the Corinthians in regard to their misuse of the Lord's Supper will help us to understand. It is, says Paul, because they behaved so badly at the Supper that many are weak and ill, and some have died. When a man was handed over to Satan, or to the gods of the underworld, the hope was that he would be so afflicted with illness that he would repent, that, as Paul says, his flesh would be destroyed, but his spirit saved. It is very significant that in the Second Letter to the Corinthians (2 Corinthians 2. 5–10) we find Paul pleading for sympathetic treatment for the man who had been delivered to Satan, so that he may not be driven to despair but may be forgiven and comforted in love. It is clear that all discipline, even the delivering of a man to Satan, was meant for the man's amendment. The aim was not obliteration; it was restoration. If a man was banished from the fellowship for a time, it was only to restore him to it, a better Christian, in the end.

The history of authority within the Church and of its

accompanying discipline falls into certain well-marked stages.

In the first stage authority within the Church was a personal matter. Authority centred round certain people, partly because of the power of their personality, and even more because of their connection with Jesus during the days of his earthly ministry. So we find Peter acting as the leader and director of the Church, when the Christians met to find a replacement for Judas (Acts 1. 15). We find James taking a leading part in deciding the Church's policy in regard to the Gentiles (Acts 15. 13). We have already seen the influence of the congregation at such moments, but the moving leadership is not the leadership of anybody, of Church officials; the leadership is a personal matter.

We can see this at its highest point in the letters of Paul. Paul makes his decisions and issues his warnings and commands on his own personal authority. True, at the beginning of his ministry he had gone to Jerusalem to receive, as it were, the *imprimatur* of the Church on his gospel and his work (Galatians 2. 1–10), and it was his custom to report to the Church what he had done (Acts 14. 27; 15. 2; 21. 19). It was not that Paul acted as if the Church as a whole did not exist, but when it was a matter of dealing with the congregations he had founded, he did so on his own personal authority. Nor was Paul ever afraid of the word 'I'. 'I Paul say to you' (Galatians 5. 2). 'I Paul myself entreat you' (2 Corinthians 10. 1). 'I warned those who sinned before and all the others, and I warn them now' (2 Corinthians 13. 2). He speaks of 'the things which we command' (2 Thessalonians 3. 4, 6). He insists on unquestioning obedience to what he says (2 Corinthians 2. 9). He is ready to punish every disobedience (2 Corinthians 10. 6). The congregation is warned to have nothing to do with anyone who will not accept the authority of Paul (2 Thessalonians 3. 14). 'I say,' he writes quite simply, that is, 'My advice is' (1 Corinthians 7. 8,

35). 'About the other things I will give you directions when I come' (1 Corinthians 11. 34). There is no hesitating and self-deprecating about Paul's way of speaking. That he says a thing is enough.

There are certain things upon which this authority is founded. It is founded on the fact that he is an apostle. 'I Paul an apostle,' he begins his letter to the Galatians (Galatians 1. 1; cp. 1 Corinthians 1. 1; 2 Corinthians 1. 1). Apostleship gives him a right to speak. It is founded on the consciousness of a call from God. God called him through his grace (Galatians 1. 15). He is called to be an apostle (Romans 1. 1). His authority is not self-assumed, nor is his apostleship; it is a matter of destiny. He is God-appointed. He is approved by God (1 Thessalonians 2. 4). He is commissioned by God (1 Corinthians 3. 10). He is entrusted with the message of God, and is the ambassador of Christ (2 Corinthians 5. 19, 20). It is by the will of God that he is an apostle (Ephesians 1. 1; Colossians 1. 1), and it is a divine office that has been given to him (Colossians 1. 25). It is because of the grace given to him that he has the right to speak (Romans 12. 3; 15. 15).

This gives Paul the sense that, when he speaks, his authority comes not from himself, but from the fact that he is speaking for God or Jesus. 'We have the mind of Christ,' he says (1 Corinthians 2. 16). 'In my judgment,' he says, 'and I think I have the spirit of God' (1 Corinthians 7. 40). 'What I am writing to you is a command of the Lord' (1 Corinthians 14. 37). God is making his appeal through him (2 Corinthians 5. 20). 'Christ is speaking in me' (2 Corinthians 13. 3). He speaks of the authority which the Lord has given him (2 Corinthians 13. 10). This is made even more impressive from the fact that there are some few cases where Paul says that he is speaking on his own. 'I say, not the Lord,' he writes to the Corinthians in the chapter on marriage problems (1 Corinthians 7. 12). 'I have no command of the Lord, but I give my opinion' (1 Corinthians 7. 25). Paul's authority comes from the fact that he is conscious for the most part of being the mouthpiece of the divine voice.

Paul cites the authority of the tradition of the Church. 'Hold to the traditions which you were taught by us' (2 Thessalonians 2. 15). The words which Paul uses for *receiving* and *delivering* are the technical words for giving and receiving an oral tradition, and he uses these words in connection with the observance of the Lord's Supper and in connection with the evidence for the Resurrection (1 Corinthians 11. 23; 15. 1, 3). In the Pastoral Epistles a word is used which would paint a vivid picture to the mind of a Greek. 'Guard,' he says, 'what has been entrusted to you' (1 Timothy 6. 20; 2 Timothy 2. 2). The Greek word for *that which has been entrusted* is *parathēkē*, a deposit, and to the Greek it was one of the most sacred duties in all life to hand back complete and uninjured a deposit which had been entrusted. So the Church has a tradition. and that tradition has a very special authority.

There is the authority of Scripture. 'All scripture inspired by God is also profitable for teaching, for reproof, for correction, and for training in righteousness' (2 Timothy 3. 16). In Romans 9–11 there are no fewer than twenty-eight citations from the Old Testament. But the interpretation of Scripture must be within the Church. 'No prophecy of Scripture is a matter of one's own interpretation.' In the hands of the ignorant and the unstable man Scripture can be twisted to his own destruction (2 Peter 1. 20, 21; 3. 16). A man's interpretation of Scripture must be within the tradition of the Church, and in a sense, while it is true that a man's call comes from God, there is a special gift and a special accrediting which come to him through his ordination by the Church (2 Timothy 1. 6; 4. 14). The individual is not on his own; he is within the Church. There is a real sense in which it is true that a man cannot have God to be his father unless he has the Church to be his mother.

All this consciousness of divine authority did not turn the Christian into a political anarchist or revolutionary, for the first Christians recognised and accepted the authority of the state. Jesus had laid it down as a principle that his followers should render to Caesar the things that are Caesar's and to God the things that are God's (Matthew 22. 15–22). That is to say the Christian must meticulously fulfil his duties both as a Christian and as a citizen. Paul regarded the state as a divine institution. 'Let every person be subject to the governing authorities, for there is no authority except from God, and those that exist have been instituted by God. Therefore he who resists the authorities resists what God has appointed, and those who resist will incur judgment.' The good and law-abiding citizen has nothing to fear (Romans 13. 1–7). 'Remind them,' says the letter to Titus, 'to be submissive to rulers and authorities' (Titus 3. 1). The Church is to remember in its prayers kings and all who are in high positions (1 Timothy 2. 2). There is in the second letter to the Thessalonians a cryptic reference to the power which holds the mystery of evil in check, and one possible explanation is that that power is the Roman Empire (2 Thessalonians 2. 7). Paul may well have seen in the *Pax Romana*, the Roman peace, established throughout the world, the one restraint which kept the world from disintegrating into chaos. Peter gives the same advice to his people: 'Be subject for the Lord's sake to every human institution, whether it be to the emperor as supreme, or to governors as sent by him to punish those who do wrong and to praise those who do right ... Honour all men. Love the brotherhood. Fear God. Honour the emperor' (1 Peter 2. 13–17).

It is at first sight an extraordinary thing to remember that, when Paul urged obedience to the state, and when Peter urged honour for the emperor, the emperor was in fact Nero, whose name has become a byword for evil. But it has to be remembered that in the early years of his

reign Nero left the government of his empire to the
philosopher Seneca and the soldier Burrus, and that men
spoke of these years as the Golden Quinquennium, the five
year period when government was at its best and greatest.

In only one New Testament book is there any other
attitude to the state, and that is the Revelation. There
Rome is the great harlot, drunk with the blood of the
saints and the martyrs (Revelation 17. 1–6). The Revelation was written in the days when persecution had
broken out, when the Roman emperor had been made a
god and when all men had to worship him and to burn
their pinch of incense to his godhead once a year as a
token of their loyalty. Revelation comes from the days
when the choice was Caesar or Christ. These were extraordinary times. In all ordinary times the Church taught
that it was a Christian duty to be a good citizen and to
accept the authority of the state.

That certain men have this personal authority there is
no doubt. In *The Curious Diversity* which tells the story
of the last hundred years in the history of Glasgow University there is told the story of the rectorial address of
December 1879. The person remembering is Sir John
Mann and the Rector of the University was W. E. Gladstone. Gladstone was given the usual stormy reception.
'He stood impassive,' says Sir John, 'high above the
tumult, awaiting the end of the din, while professor after
professor appealed with uplifted hands for silence.' After
a long time – twenty minutes according to another who
was there – Gladstone decided that there had been
enough noise. 'I vividly recall,' says Sir John, 'how he
merely raised his hand and said, "Gentlemen". Immediately there was silence.' That is authority, personal
authority which has nothing to do with any office or
position.

So in the very early days Peter and James and Paul had
this personal authority, long before any institutional or
administrative structure had entered into the life of the

Church. This was natural in the first days of the Church, but it was clearly a situation which could not last. It was bound to come to an end, because these great leaders must pass from the scene, and because the bigger the Church became the less it could depend on the presence of exceptional men and the more it came to heed some kind of organisation to control its day-to-day affairs. So the age of Church office-bearers succeeded the period of personal authority.

The simplest division in the leadership of the Church is the division between those who were itinerant and whose writ ran throughout the whole Church, those whose ministry had a universal character, and those whose ministry was exercised in one place, those whose ministry was congregational and local. Even in Paul's earliest letters there are indications that local leadership was there. He writes to the Thessalonian Church: 'We beseech you, brethren, to respect those who labour among you and *are over you in the Lord,* and admonish you, and to esteem them very highly because of their work' (1 Thessalonians 5. 12, 13). In the long list of gifts in the first letter to the Corinthians we find *helpers* and *administrators* listed (1 Corinthians 12. 28). In the last chapter of the same letter Paul refers to Stephanas and his household and says: 'I urge you *to be subject* to such men' (1 Corinthians 16. 16). Every congregation must have inevitably produced its leaders.

We begin with the men whose ministry was exercised throughout the whole Church. Every list of office-bearers begins in the same way – with the apostles and prophets (1 Corinthians 12. 28; Ephesians 4. 11; 3. 5). It is on the foundation of the apostles and prophets that the Church is built (Ephesians 2. 20). The apostles and the prophets were the men whose ministry was not confined to one place, but was exercised throughout the whole Church; they had in the earliest days a universal authority. So it is natural to begin with them.

Apo means *out* and *stellein* means *to send*; *apostolos* therefore means *a person or an expedition sent out.* *Apostolos* in Greek can mean a naval squadron; it can mean a messenger, sent, for example, with a legal instruction or demand; and, for our purposes above all, it can mean an *ambassador. Apostolos*, therefore, means more than simply sent out; it means sent out clothed and equipped with the authority of the sender. An *apostolos*, an apostle, does not speak or act for himself; he speaks and acts for the person who sent him.

The corresponding Hebrew word is *sheliach*, which means *a commissioned representative.* A *sheliach* can represent the sender, for instance, in arrangements for the payment of a debt, or in arrangements for the carrying out of a divorce action. At the Sabbath Synagogue service one of the congregation was chosen to say the prayers, and he was known as the *sheliach zibbur*, the representative of the congregation towards God. So on the Day of Atonement the High Priest was the *sheliach* of the nation. In the days of the Jewish Diaspora, the days when the Jews were scattered all over the world, the Sanhedrin sent its rulings and decisions to them by means of a *sheliach.* So Paul when he went to root out the Christians of Damascus was the *sheliach*, the apostle, of the Sanhedrin, with letters of authorisation from the Sanhedrin (Acts 9. 2). So in the Hebrew *sheliach* there was the same characteristic as there was in the Greek *apostolos.* Both are representatives of a power greater than themselves, and both are equipped with the authority of the sender.

So then the apostle is the representative, the commissioned envoy, the ambassador of Jesus Christ; he speaks for his Master and is clad with the power of his Master. The word *apostolos* occurs three times in the New Testament in its secular sense, and these occurrences illustrate its meaning. 'A servant is not greater than his master; nor is the *apostolos*, he who is sent, greater than he who sent him' (John 13. 16). Epaphroditus is the *apostolos*, the messenger, of the Philippian Church to Paul (Philippians 2. 25). He is their commissioned representative; he will do for them what they all wish to do for Paul. The representatives of the Churches who are to take the contributions of the Churches to the Church at Jerusalem are the messengers, the *apostoloi*, of their congregations (2 Corinthians 8. 23). In every case the *apostolos* carries out a duty on behalf of, and in the name of, him who sent him.

This explains the qualification of an apostle. When a new apostle is to be chosen to replace Judas, Peter says: 'So one of the men who have accompanied us during all the time that the Lord Jesus went in and out among us, beginning from the baptism of John until the day when he was taken up from us – one of these men must become with us a witness to his resurrection' (Acts 1. 21, 22). The qualification of the apostle was that he must have personal knowledge of the earthly and the risen Lord. This means that the apostles will be mainly the original Twelve. Already in the New Testament the title apostle is occasionally used of some few outside the Twelve. Paul uses it regularly of himself (e.g., 1 Corinthians 15. 9). Matthias was enrolled among the apostles as the replacement for Judas (Acts 1. 26). James the brother of our Lord was an apostle, and was indeed the head of the Jerusalem Church (Galatians 1. 19; Acts 12. 17; 15. 13; 21. 17–26). Andronicus and Junias, about whom nothing whatever is known, were apostles (Romans 16. 7). It is just possible that the second name should be not Junias but Junia, which is a feminine name, in which case a woman is designated an apostle. Barnabas was an apostle (Acts 14. 4, 14). This leaves three doubtful cases. There is the case of Timothy and Silvanus. Timothy and Silvanus are associated with Paul in the writing of the first letter to the Thessalonians (1 Thessalonians 1. 1); and later in the letter Paul writes: 'We might have made demands as the apostles of Christ.' Who is the *we*? If it is intended to include Timothy and Silvanus, then they were apostles; if Paul is referring to himself (the royal or editorial we), then they were not. The one remaining possibility is Apollos. In the first letter to the Corinthians Paul writes: 'I have applied all this to myself and Apollos.' And then a little later he goes on: 'I think that God has exhibited us apostles as last of all, like men sentenced to death' (1 Corinthians 4. 6, 9). There must be a question-mark against the names of Timothy, Silvanus and Apollos, with the probability that they were not apostles. Later, the title apostle was used in a wider sense for the missionary emissaries of the Church sent out to evangelise and to convert. But apostle was a title which vanished early from the Church – we shall later see why; and apostleship never became an office in the organisational and institutional structure of the Church.

Second only to the apostles there came the prophets; they too had as their sphere the whole Church. The word prophet, *prophētēs*, means *one who speaks for another*. In the human sense it can be used for someone who expounds and explains a master's teaching. In the divine sense the Greeks called both Apollo the god, and Tiresias the mortal, the interpreter, the *prophētēs*, of Zeus. A. F. Kirkpatrick defines the Hebrew use of the word: 'The prophet is the spokesman or interpreter of God, one who is the medium through which divine revelations are made.' Since Moses is not a good speaker himself, Aaron is to be his prophet (Exodus 7. 1). Aaron is to be a mouth for Moses as the old story so vividly puts it (Exodus 4. 16). So the prophet is a mouth for God. As Kirkpatrick puts it a little more fully: 'Primitive Christian prophecy is the inspired speech of charismatic preachers, through whom God's plan of salvation for the world and the community, and his will for the life of the individual Christian, are shown.' Prophecy was a main activity in the early Church. There are certain things to be noted.

i. Prophecy by the definition of it already given is forthtelling far more than it is foretelling; it is proclamation rather than prediction. The element of foretelling is not completely absent. The prophet Agabus at Antioch foretold the coming famine (Acts 11. 27, 28), and later at Caesarea he foretold what was to happen to Paul in Jerusalem (Acts 21. 10, 11). But prediction is not a main part of New Testament prophecy; proclamation is.

ii. As the Jews saw it, with Malachi the days of prophecy came to an end. The Psalmist writes wistfully: 'There is no longer any prophet, and there is none among us who knows how long' (Psalm 74. 9). In the time of the Maccabees they did not know what to do with the altar which had been profaned, so they stored the stones 'until there should come a prophet to tell us what to do with them' (1 Maccabees 4. 46). At a time of lawlessness in Israel after the death of Judas Maccabaeus it is said: 'Thus there was great distress in Israel, such as had not been since the time that the prophets ceased to appear among them' (1 Maccabees 9. 27). The Jews decide that Simon should be permanent leader and high priest, 'until a trustworthy prophet should arise' (1 Maccabees 14. 41). For the Jews prophecy was at an end. But in the New Testament the prophets are mentioned no fewer than one hundred and forty-four times. They occur everywhere – Rome (Romans 12. 6, 7); Corinth (1 Corinthians 14. 32, 37, 39); Thessalonica (1 Thessalonians 5. 20); Antioch (Acts 13. 1); Caesarea (Acts 21. 9, 10). This was indeed the proof that the new age, when 'your sons and your daughters will prophesy' (Joel 2. 28), had come. One of the great distinguishing marks of Christianity was the rebirth of prophecy.

iii. The hall-mark of prophecy is intelligibility. It is precisely this that Paul stresses when he is comparing prophecy and speaking with tongues in 1 Corinthians 14. Anyone can understand and profit by what the prophet says (1 Corinthians 14. 4, 24, 25). No one can understand

what speaking with tongues means; the whole performance can look like bedlam (1 Corinthians 14. 2, 6–12, 16,
23). Therefore prophecy is much to be preferred and
sought after (1 Corinthians 14. 5, 19, 39). Prophecy is the
plain proclamation of the message of God, and therefore
it speaks with authority.

iv. The prophets were given a special independence.
The Teaching of the Twelve Apostles, the *Didachē*, lays
down the right order for the celebration of the Eucharist,
but it finishes by saying: 'Let the prophets hold Eucharist as they will' (Didachē 10. 7). The prophet was above
the ordinary regulations.

It is easy to see how great an authority the apostle and
the prophet would have, because the very essence of both
of them was that they were in direct contact with God,
and when they spoke it was the voice of God. And yet by
the end of the first century both were on the way out.
Why should that be so?

i. It was so in the nature of things. This was specially
so in the case of the apostle. It is true that the title
apostle was used to describe an envoy sent out by the
Church on a missionary task, a pioneer of Christianity in
places where the name of Jesus had not been told. But in
the beginning an apostle had been a man who had
known Jesus in our Lord's earthly ministry and who had
been a witness of the Resurrection. Clearly, such men
were a vanishing and irreplaceable body. When the original apostles died, there were none, and there could be
none, to take their place.

ii. Apostles and prophets were front-line troops, and,
in the days when persecution came, casualties among
them were very high. They had a special prominence in
the ministry of the Church, and the death rate among
them was high. The apostle and the prophet tended to
become the martyr.

iii. Apostles and prophets tended as time went on to
become anachronisms. The stronger the local and settled

ministry became, the less place there was for these itinerant wanderers. We can see the clash happening in the
little third letter of John. John begins by praising the
journeying strangers and pleading for their support (3
John 5–8). He goes on to condemn Diotrephes, for refusing
to accept his, John's authority, for refusing to welcome
the wandering strangers, and for doing his best to stop
others from welcoming them. Diotrephes is clearly the
settled head of the local congregation, and he finds it
something of a nuisance and something of a menace
when his congregation is invaded by these itinerant
preachers, and, as far as he is concerned, John is an aged
anachronism who would be well to stop interfering with
the local arrangements (3 John 9, 10). Apparently there
was another Church leader called Demetrius who was
more amenable to the authority of the ancient apostle and
the activities of the wandering prophets. Here is the clash
between John the aged apostle, claiming an authority
which the local ministry were no longer willing to give
him, the clash between the wandering prophets and the
local ministry to whom the arrival of the prophets was no
more than an undesirable disturbance, the clash between
the old set-up in which the apostle and prophet were
supreme and the new set-up in which the essence of the
Church was in the local congregation and the settled
ministry.

It is a clash which is still liable to happen to this day.
Howard Williams tells in his book *My Word*: 'I recall an
evangelist visiting my church in the early days of my ministry who announced in the vestibule after a surprisingly
sudden harvest: "There! I have won these young people
for Christ. Now look after them." I viewed his enterprise
with a cynical eye and I am still unashamed to do so after
a number of years.' Once the authority of the local congregation was established the authority of the itinerant
apostle and prophet could never be the same.

iv. Great as the apostolic and prophetic ministry was,

it was nevertheless singularly liable to abuse. *The Teaching of the Twelve Apostles*, the *Didachē* dates to about A.D. 100; it is the earliest book of Church Order, and it lays down very significant rules for the treatment of the apostles and prophets. 'Concerning the Apostles and Prophets, act thus according to the ordinance of the Gospel. Let every Apostle who comes to you be received as the Lord, but let him not stay more than one day, or if need be a second as well; but if he stays three days he is a false prophet. And when an Apostle goes forth, let him accept nothing but bread till he reaches his night's lodging; but if he asks for money he is a false prophet.' The regulations continue: 'Not everyone who speaks in a spirit is a prophet, except he has the behaviour of the Lord. From his behaviour, then, the false prophet and the true prophet shall be known. And no prophet who orders a meal in a spirit shall eat of it; otherwise he is a false prophet. And every prophet who teaches the truth; if he does not do what he teaches, is a false prophet ... But whoever shall say in a spirit: "Give me money or something else," you shall not listen to him; but if he tells you to give for the benefit of others in want, let none judge him' (*Didachē* 11. 3–12).

It is easy to see what was sometimes happening. In the very early days the apostle and the prophet had a very considerable, even a unique prestige; and it was not difficult for less scrupulous men to cash in on this, and to find for themselves a not uncomfortable living at the expense of the Christian communities. No one is suggesting that this was common, but that the *Didachē* finds it worthwhile to legislate against it shows that it did happen.

That the Christians were simple, gullible folk was noticed even by the heathen. Lucian in his essay *The Passing of Peregrinus* describes the career of quackery and fraud of Peregrinus. In the end justice caught up with him, but he had so imposed upon the Christians that they treated him as a glorious martyr and showered comfort and help and gifts upon. Lucian says that they had been taught to love all men and to despise all earthly property. 'So if any charlatan or trickster, able to profit by occasions, comes among them, he quickly acquires sudden wealth by imposing upon simple folk.' So, says Lucian, until even the Christians found him out, this impostor roamed about, 'possessing an ample source of funds in the Christians, through whose ministrations he lived in unalloyed prosperity. For a time he battened himself thus upon them.' Even the heathen could see that it was easy to take advantage of the Christians who were sometimes too lovingly trusting for this wicked world, and sometimes there were alleged Christians who found in the itinerant ministry an easy life. So bit by bit the itinerant ministry came to its end and left the local settled ministry supreme, and it is to it and to its authority that we must now turn.

In the first stage there was an authority which was based on personal qualities. In the second stage there was an authority whose limits were extended throughout the whole Church. Now at the third stage we arrive at the local ministry which was to become the settled, universal and established seat of authority within the Church. In the set-up of the New Testament Church we find the deacon, the elder and the bishop.

The deacon was the lower office, but the very word *deacon* has in it the very essence of Christianity, and the basic distinction between the Christian and the non-Christian way of life. The word *deacon* comes from the Greek verb *diakonein* which means *to serve*. Beyer gives a most illuminating treatment of the word in *The Theological Dictionary of the New Testament*, edited in German by G. Kittel, and translated into English by G. W. Bromiley. From the beginning there is a concrete, practical air about *diakonein*; it basically indicates personal service. So it can be used of waiting at table, more generally of care and concern to provide for others, and for the work of a woman in the house and home. This kind of service did not at all stand high in Greek eyes. Plato (*Gorgias* 491 E) quotes the saying of the Sophist: 'How can a man be happy when he has to serve someone?' Service is regarded as 'slavish and illiberal'. True, the word can move up to mean service of the state and even service of the gods. But the Greek was an individualist. He did not want to serve others; he wanted to develop himself. As Beyer says: 'For the Greek in his freedom and wisdom there can certainly be no question of existing to serve others.'

The Jew saw nothing objectionable or mean about service. Had he not been told to love his neighbour as himself? (Leviticus 19. 18). But in later Judaism the idea of service had less to do with love than with the idea of winning merit for oneself – and in any event service was not to be given to the unrighteous.

Christianity transformed the whole idea of service. In the New Testament *diakonein* still means to wait at table (John 12. 2) or to supervise the service of meals (Acts 6. 2). But in the Christian view of life service comes to be a summary of 'the whole action of Christian love to others'. The very word is an assumption of the obligation to serve others, a service which may end, as it did for Jesus, in the ultimate sacrifice. The Christian charter of service is in the saying of Jesus: 'You know that those who are supposed to rule over the Gentiles lord it over them, and their great men exercise authority over them. But it shall not be so among you; but whoever would be great among you must be your servant, and whoever would be first among you must be the slave of all. For the Son of Man also came not to be served but to serve, and to give his life a ransom for many' (Mark 10. 42–45; cp. Luke 22. 24–27; and the action of Jesus in John 13. 3–5).

Here then is the magnificent background of the word *diakonos*, deacon. Clearly, the duty of the deacon will have to do with the administration of the Church and the practical service of the Church's members. In the New Testament the deacon first appears in the address of the letter to the Philippians (1. 1). In the Pastoral Epistles the deacon is spoken of immediately after the bishop, and his qualifications are listed in 1 Timothy 3. 8–13. He is to be serious, not double-tongued, not addicted to wine, not greedy for gain; he is to hold the mystery of the faith with a clear conscience; he is to be tested; he is to be the husband of one wife and he is to be a good parent and the maker of a good home.

The New Testament itself has nothing to say about the actual duties of the deacon; but the later Church Canons, such as the Canons of Hippolytus, define his duties. He is the official who is responsible for the subordinate services of the Church. He is to be the servant of God, the servant of the bishop, and the servant of the elders. He is to visit the congregation, and he is to report cases of illness to the elders and to the bishop. He is to have special charge of the poor, of widows, of orphans and of strangers. He is to instruct catechumens and to report when they are ready for baptism. He is the bishop's almoner and is to care for clergy who happen to be in need. He is to share with the bishop in the administration of Church funds. He is forbidden to have anything to do with worldly business, unless he has been appointed the legal guardian of an orphan. He is forbidden to serve in the army, to accept either military or civil office, to become security for anyone, or to exact usury from anyone. He is forbidden to enter or to eat in a tavern, unless he is on a journey.

Within the New Testament itself there is no difference between the elder, the *presbuteros*, and the bishop, the *episkopos*. Jerome writes: 'Among the ancients bishops and presbyters are the same, for the one is a term of dignity, the other of age.' That the two terms describe the same person emerges from the following facts: i. Philippians is addressed to the bishops and deacons (Philippians 1. 1). If there had been a separate body of elders they could hardly have been omitted; ii. In 1 Timothy 3 where the bishop and the deacons are described, there is no mention of the elders, and yet unquestionably there were elders in the Church to which the letter was written for in 1 Timothy 5. 17 it is stated that the elders who rule well are to be accounted worthy of double honour; iii. Titus 1. 5 begins by speaking about elders and Titus 1. 7 passes without comment into instructions about bishops, and it is clear that the same persons are being spoken about; iv. Acts 20. 17 tells how Paul summoned the elders of Ephesus to come to see him, the *presbuteroi*, and in Acts 20. 28 these same people are called overseers, *episkopoi*. In the same passage the words *presbuteroi* and *episkopoi* are applied to the same people; v. In 1 Peter 5. 1 elders are addressed, *presbuteroi,* and in verse 2 they are urged to tend, *episkopein*, the flock. The duty of an elder is to act as an *episkopos*. The distinction is that *presbuteros* describes the person involved personally; he is an older person. *Episkopos* describes him from the point of view of his function; his function is to oversee, superintend, the flock of the Church. Let us then look at the two terms separately.

Elder is the oldest existing title of honour. Age was always held in respect. The Greek governing body was the *gerousia*, and *gerōn* is the Greek for an old man. The Latin governing body was the *senatus*, and *senex* is the Latin for an old man. In English the *alderman* and in Arabic the *shiek* are simply the older men. We find the elders everywhere. We find them in Egypt (Genesis 50. 7), and in Moab and Midian (Numbers 22. 7). We find them in Israel at all stages in Israel's history. They are there even in the days of slavery in Egypt (Exodus 3. 16); in the wilderness journeyings (Exodus 19. 7); at the giving of the commandments (Exodus 24. 1). They are there to relieve and support Moses in the duties of leadership (Numbers 11. 16). When the people reach the Promised Land the elders are the purveyors of justice (Deuteronomy 19.

12; 22. 15). They have to do with the cities of refuge
(Joshua 20. 4). They are the protectors of the rights of the
people (Judges 8. 14; Ruth 4. 2). They take the lead in
the choice of a king (1 Samuel 8. 4, 5), and are involved in
intrigues with David (1 Samuel 30. 26), and with the
plans of Jezebel (1 Kings 21. 8–11). On the return from
exile they are involved in the rebuilding of the city and
in the issue of proclamations (Ezra 6. 7; 10. 8). In New
Testament times they are the directors of the Synagogue
and they form a section of the Sanhedrin, and therefore
play a leading part in the arrest and the death of Jesus
(Matthew 16. 21; 21. 23; 26. 3, 47, 57, 59; 27. 1, 3, 12, 20,
41). In the earliest days of the Church they are connected
with the relief of the poor (Acts 11. 30). All over the East
and all through the history of Israel the elders play a
leading part.

No less are the elders prominent in the Graeco-Roman
world. In Sparta the elders were the presiding officers of
the various state boards and councils. In Egypt we find
that each trade had its elders and so we find the elders of
the cultivators and the elders of the fishermen. We find
that the elder is in charge of the good order of the village,
and is responsible for the maintenance of the public
peace. And even in the temples we find elder priests who
are in charge of the administration.

The fact is that it would have been an astonishment if
the Church had not had elders, for in the ancient world
and all over it the elder was the leader of the community
in things secular and in things spiritual. We shall leave
the consideration of the qualifications of the elder until
we come to the bishop, for they are the same for both.
Here we collect what information there is in the New
Testament about the activities of the elders. They are
said to have been appointed in every congregation (Acts
14. 23; Titus 1. 5), which is exactly what we would expect.
The Jerusalem elders received and no doubt administered the gifts brought for poor relief (Acts 11. 30). In

James we read that the elders visited the sick and
anointed them and prayed for them (James 5. 14). The
elders clearly had a large part in the administration of
the congregation and the leadership of the people. They
are there at the Council of Jerusalem when the door was
opened to the Gentiles (Acts 15. 4, 6, 22, 23); they are
present with James to receive the report of Paul (Acts 21.
18). It is their duty to tend, to oversee the flock (Acts 20.
28; 1 Peter 5. 1–4). In the ancient world the elders were
the backbone of every community, and it was so in the
Church.

The third of the words for the permanent local officials
of the Church was the word bishop, *episkopos*. The word
episkopos came to the service of the Christian Church
with a great history. *Epi* in this case means *over*, and
skopein means *to see*; so *episkopos* is one who oversees.
From there the word goes on to mean one who oversees in
such a way that he is a *guardian* or a *protector*; and so
the word ends up with the idea of overseeing people with
gracious care and concern.

On the Greek side the word has a divine aspect. In
Homer (*Iliad* 22. 254, 255) the gods are the overseers, the
episkopoi, the guardians of pledges and treaties, thus
safeguarding their inviolability. In Aeschylus (*Seven
against Thebes* 271) the gods are the *episkopoi*, the protectors of the city, the countryside and the market-place
alike. Demosthenes (*Oration* 421) speaks of the goddess
Athenē holding her hands over Athens as an *episkopos*, as
its guardian and protector. Plutarch (*Greek Questions*
47) tells that the goddess Artemis is the *episkopos*, the
guardian of pregnant women. In a second century papyrus
the Furies are said to be the *episkopoi*, the protectors, of
graves, and so all are warned that a grave can only be
violated at the risk of the vengeance of the Furies.

Beyer in Kittel's *Theological Dictionary of the New
Testament* goes on to trace the human side of *episkopos*.
In Plato's *Laws* (762 D) the officials called the Guardians

are to be the *episkopoi*, the watchers to see that no law is transgressed. Plutarch in his life of Solon (19) tells how Solon set up an assembly to be the *episkopos*, the watcher over all things, and the guardian of the laws. In the *Laws* (784 A) Plato lays it down that older and maturer women should be the *episkopoi*, the advisers to young married couples; and he provides for the appointment of market *episkopoi*, superintendents, who will watch for fair and unfair dealing (849 A).

The word *episkopos* already had certain official uses. From Athens *episkopoi*, perhaps governors would be the meaning, were sent to the member cities of the Attic League to keep the public order and to maintain right relations with Athens. Arrian in *The History of India* (12. 5) tells how Alexander in the conquered areas installed *episkopoi*, who were to act somewhat as secret police. There were *episkopoi*, superintendents in charge of poor relief, of public morals, of civic administration. In Rhodes there were administrative temple officials called *episkopoi*, and in Syria the *episkopoi* were supervisors of buildings, of public works, and of temple and public funds.

In the Greek world both in its divine use and its human use *episkopos* was already a very great word.

On the Jewish side *episkopos* is almost as great. It is used of God. In *Wisdom* (1. 6) God is *panepiskopos*, the one who sees and watches all, and in particular the human heart. In the Greek Old Testament the word is used for military section officers (Numbers 31. 14; 2 Kings 11. 15); for building superintendents (2 Chronicles 34. 12, 17); for temple overseers (Nehemiah 11. 9, 14, 22); and for the person who had charge of the temple oil and incense, cereals for the offerings, oil for anointing, the sanctuary and its vessels (Numbers 4. 16).

Jeremias in *Jerusalem in the Time of Jesus* (pp. 260, 261) finds a possible model for the Christian *episkopos* in the *mebaqqēr* of the Covenanter Communities who had their main centre at Qumran. At the head of each camp there was a supervisor called a *mebaqqēr*, a superintendent. He must be between thirty and fifty years of age. He must be an expert in the Law. All transgressions had to be reported to him. He alone could admit candidates to the community, and he examined and classified new recruits. He was the spiritual father of the community. Like a father he pitied his sons; like a shepherd he tended his sheep. It was his duty to see that none in the community was oppressed or beaten, and he 'loosed all the fetters that tie them'. He received and distributed charitable gifts. Whether or not this official had anything to do with the development of the Chrisian *episkopos*, his functions in the community were the same. Another suggestion is that the model of the Christian bishop is to be found in the *archisunagōgos*, the ruler or president of the Synagogue. This official was not himself personally responsible for the preaching or the worship, but he was responsible for the whole administration of the Synagogue and for seeing to it that the Synagogue affairs were in good order, and the Synagogue services correctly and reverently carried out. He too may have played his part in the build-up of the idea of the Christian bishop.

Episkopos occurs in the New Testament only five times. In 1 Peter 2. 25 it is applied to Jesus, and Jesus is called the Shepherd and Guardian (*episkopos*) of your souls. In Acts 20. 28 Paul tells the Ephesian elders that the Holy Spirit has made them overseers (*episkopoi*) to care for the Church of God. The letter to the Philippians is addressed to the bishops (*episkopoi*) and deacons (Philippians 1. 1). The R.S.V. in the margin suggests overseers as an alternative translation. The two main New Testament passages about bishops are 1 Timothy 3. 1–7 and Titus 1. 3–9. There the qualifications of a bishop are set out. He must possess certain *personal and moral* qualities; he must be above reproach, temperate, sensible, dignified, no drunkard, not violent, gentle, not quarrelsome, no lover of money. He must have certain *professional* qualities; he must be a skilled teacher. He must have certain *social* qualities; he must be a hospitable person. One of the problems of the ancient world was the fact that inns were notoriously dirty, expensive and immoral. The bishop therefore had to be a man ready and willing to keep open house and home for Christians who were on journeys or who were strangers in a strange place. He must have certain *domestic* qualities; his household must be an exemplary home, and he must have full parental control over his family. He must have certain *public* qualities; he must not be a newcomer to the Church; too quick advancement could well beget an ugly conceit; and he must be well thought of and respected by people outside the Church. The early Church was well aware that its ministers, simply because they were ministers, were automatically Public Relations Officers for the Church and for Christianity. It is plain to see that the qualifications of the bishop have little to do with his academic status and have everything to do with the impact that his life and personality are going to make on the community both outside and inside the congregation.

Such then is the authority of the Church within New Testament times. It has three stages. It begins with a brief time when authority was located in the outstanding personalities of those who had been with Jesus in the days of his earthly ministry. It moved on to a second stage when authority specially belonged to the apostles and prophets, whose writ ran throughout the whole Church. It ended in the third stage, which became the final set-up, in which authority was vested in the permanent officials of the local Church, in the deacons, the elders and the bishops, always remembering that at this stage the elders and the bishops were the same people.

Chapter 5

Authority in the Church
After the New Testament

The bigger the Church became, the more difficult became
the twin problems of authority and discipline. So long as
the Church was a small body, so long as each congregation was a mere handful of people, authority and discipline could be handled as almost a family affair. But
when the Church expanded, when its numbers grew ever
larger, when it became a worldwide institution, then the
problem of authority and discipline became a very different thing. When Church membership was small, the
members consisted practically entirely of committed and
dedicated Christians; but the larger the membership, the
more members there were who were only loosely attached
to the Church, and whose commitment did not go very
deep. In the very early days of the Church, as Paul wrote
to the Corinthians, there were not many wise by worldly
standards, not many powerful, not many of noble birth (1
Corinthians 1. 26), but when the Church began to spread
throughout all levels of society, into the Church there
came people with sophisticated minds and seeking intel-
lects. Religion itself ceased to be enough; theology was
born. And heresy is always the price of thought. The result
of all this was a situation in which authority and discipline
became ever more necessary and ever more difficult. At
that situation I now wish to look. It is not possible to
write a history of authority and discipline within the
Church. What we will do is to look at certain key figures

and certain particularly important periods in the development of authority and discipline in the Church.

The first name to stand out is the name of Ignatius. Ignatius was the third bishop of Antioch in Syria. He was condemned to be sent to Rome to be killed by the beasts in the arena. The journey was made by way of certain Churches in Asia Minor, and as he went to death he wrote his letters. At Smyrna he wrote to Ephesus, to Magnesia, to Tralles and to Rome. Later, from Troas, he wrote to Philadelphia, to Smyrna and to Polycarp. All this happened within the reign of Trajan (A.D. 98–117), and it was sometime about A.D. 112 when Ignatius won the martyr's crown.

No martyr ever more willingly embraced death. He speaks of the privilege of fighting with beasts at Rome, and calls his chains his spiritual pearls (*To the Ephesians* 1. 2; 11. 2). He writes to the Church at Smyrna that he has given himself to the wild beasts because 'the sword is near to God, and with the wild beasts is with God' (*To the Smyrnaeans* 4. 2). He writes almost lyrically to the Church at Rome: 'Suffer me to be eaten by the beasts, through whom I can attain to God. I am God's wheat, and I am ground by the teeth of the wild beasts that I may be found pure bread of Christ. Rather entice the wild beasts that they may become my tomb, and leave no trace of my body, that when I fall asleep I may not be burdensome to any ... I long for the beasts that are prepared for me ... Let there come on me fire, and cross, and struggles with wild beasts, cutting and tearing asunder, rackings of my bones, mangling of my limbs, crushing of my whole body, cruel tortures of the devil, if only I attain to Jesus Christ!' (*To the Romans* 5. 2, 3; 6. 1). Ignatius embraced his sufferings for through them he knew he was to embrace Jesus Christ.

The importance of Ignatius is that with him the bishop arrives full-grown on the scene. For Ignatius there were two problems and one solution.

The first of Ignatius' problems was that even thus early the menace of disunity was threatening the Church, and to Ignatius disunity was a very deadly sin. 'Be not deceived, my brothers,' he writes to the Philadelphians, 'if anyone follows a maker of schism, he does not inherit the kingdom of God' (*To the Philadelphians* 3. 3). 'Love unity,' he writes to the same Church, 'flee from divisions, be imitators of Jesus Christ, as was he also of the Father' (*To the Philadelphians* 7. 1). 'He who is within the sanctuary is pure, but he who is outside the sanctuary is not pure' (*To the Trallians* 7. 2). He writes to the Philadelphians: 'I did my best as a man who was set on unity. But where there is division and anger God does not dwell. The Lord then forgives one who repents, if his repentance leads to the unity of God' (*To the Philadelphians* 8. 1). 'Care for unity, for there is nothing better,' he writes to Polycarp (*To Polycarp* 1. 2). There are those in whom the sense of community which should characterise the Church is gone: 'Mark those who have strange opinions about the grace of Jesus Christ which has come to us, and see how contrary they are to the mind of God. They have no care for love, none for the widow, none for the orphan, none for the distressed, none for the afflicted, none for the prisoner, or for him released from prison, none for the hungry or thirsty' (*To the Smyrneans* 7. 1).

One of the terrible things about this disunity is that it may separate a man from the Eucharist, from the sacrament of the Lord's Supper, and by this time the Eucharist has become 'the medicine of immortality, the antidote that we should not die, but live for ever in Jesus Christ' (*To the Ephesians* 20. 2). Ignatius says of those in this disunity: 'They abstain from Eucharist and prayer, because they do not confess that the Eucharist is the flesh of our Saviour Jesus Christ' (*To the Smyrnaeans* 7. 1). 'Unless a man is within the sanctuary, he lacks the bread of God' (*To the Ephesians* 5. 2). 'Be careful to use one

Eucharist, for there is one flesh of our Lord Jesus Christ, and one cup for union with his blood, one altar' (*To the Philadelphians* 4. 1). He who despoils himself of the Eucharist is robbing himself of the supreme source of grace. Not only the sacrament but even marriage is to be arranged and undertaken in the unity of the Church. 'It is right for men and women who marry,' Ignatius writes to Polycarp, 'to be united with the consent of the bishop, so that the marriage may be according to the Lord and not according to lust' (*To Polycarp* 6. 1). As T. M. Lindsay writes of Ignatius in *The Church and Ministry in the Early Centuries*. 'The rallying call which rolls from the first to the last is Union! Keep united! Close the ranks!' In Ignatius there is 'a passionate anxiety that each local Church should present an unbroken front and manifest a complete unity'. It must therefore rally round its leaders, for the alternative is lawless isolation. We shall leave the solution which Ignatius offered until we have looked at his other problem.

The second problem which faced Ignatius was the problem of heresy. 'Live only on Christian fare,' he writes to the Trallians, 'and abstain from the strange food which is heresy' (*To the Trallians* 6. 1). 'If any man walks in strange doctrine, he has no part in the Passion' (*To the Philadelphians* 3. 3). Two main heresies threatened the Church.

First, there was the danger of a relapse into Judaism, or at least an acceptance of Jewish legalism. Ignatius writes to the Magnesians: 'We are no longer living for the Sabbath but for the Lord's Day.' 'It is monstrous,' he says, 'to talk of Jesus Christ and to practise Judaism' (*To the Magnesians* 9. 1; 10. 3). 'If anyone,' he writes to the Philadelphians, 'interprets Judaism to you, do not listen to him' (*To the Philadelphians* 6. 1). It took the Church a very long time to realise that Christianity was not simply a reformed version of Judaism, and that it was something new.

Second, there was an even greater threat to the faith; there was that type of thought which is known as Docetism, which is really a Greek word meaning Seemism. It will be remembered that when we spoke of Gnosticism, we saw that the basic tenet of Gnosticism is that all matter is essentially evil. If matter is essentially evil, it means that the body is evil. If the body is evil, it means that Jesus could not have had a real body. So the Gnostics, the Docetists, the Seemists, taught that Jesus had only the appearance, the semblance of a body, that he was a kind of phantom in human form, that therefore he did not really suffer and die; he merely *seemed* to suffer and die. Asia Minor was badly attacked and infected by this Docetism, this Seemism, and more than once Ignatius roundly and even passionately condemns it. He writes to the Smyrnaeans: 'What does anyone profit me, if he praises me but blasphemes my Lord, and does not confess that he was clothed in flesh?' (*To the Smyrnaeans* 5. 2). He writes of Jesus Christ 'who was *truly* born, both ate and drank, was *truly* persecuted under Pontius Pilate, was *truly* crucified and died in the sight of those in heaven and on earth and under the earth, who was *truly* raised from the dead ... But if some affirm who are without God – that is, who are unbelievers – that his suffering was only a semblance ... why am I a prisoner, and why do I even long to fight with beasts' (*To the Trallians* 9. 1, 2; 10. 1; *To the Smyrnaeans* 1. 1, 2; cp. *To the Smyrnaeans* 2. 1). 'I know and believe that he was in the flesh even after the Resurrection. And when he came to those with Peter, he said to them: "Take, handle me, and see that I am not a phantom without a body." And they immediately touched him and believed, being mingled both with his flesh and spirit ... And after his Resurrection he ate and drank with them as being of flesh, although he was united in spirit to the Father' (*To the Smyrnaeans* 3). Docetism, Seemism, would have made any doctrine of the incarnation an impossibility, and any belief in the manhood and the full humanity of Jesus beyond belief. The battle with Docetism was a battle which Ignatius had to fight – and win.

Ignatius' solution for the problems of the Church was simple and far-reaching. His solution was to make the office-bearers, the bishop, the elders and the deacons, *and especially the bishop*, the centre and the soul of the Church. It is true that he often, perhaps even usually, mentions the three sets of office-bearers together, but there is no doubt of the unique place of the bishop. The authority of the Church is epitomised and concentrated in him. Let us look at the evidence, for Ignatius started the Church on a course which certain sections of the Church never again left.

i. It is the belief of Ignatius that without these office-bearers a church does not exist. He writes to the Trallians: 'Let all respect the deacons as Jesus Christ, even as the bishop is also a type of the Father, and the presbyters as the council of God and the college of apostles. Without these the name of "church" is not given' (*To the Trallians* 3. 1). There is no Church without the basic office-bearers who represent God, Jesus and the Apostles.

ii. We may set down first of all the passage of Ignatius which most fully sets out his position. In writing to the Church at Smyrna he says: 'See that you follow the bishop as Jesus Christ follows the Father, and the Presbytery as if it was the apostles, and reverence the deacons as the command of God. Let no one do any of the things appertaining to the Church without the bishop. Let that be considered a valid Eucharist which is celebrated by the bishop, or by one whom he appoints. Wherever the bishop appears let the congregation be present, just as wherever Jesus Christ is there is the Catholic Church. It is not lawful either to baptise or to hold an Agapē (a congregational love feast) without the bishop. Whatever the bishop approves is pleasing to God, so that everything which you do may be secure and valid ... It is good to know God and the bishop. He who honours the bishop has been honoured by God; he who does anything without the knowledge of the bishop is serving the devil' (*To the Smyrnaeans* 8. 1, 2; 9. 1). The whole congregation is to revolve round the bishop. Nothing is valid without his consent and without his presence or the presence of his representative. Those who recognise the bishop in their words but deny him in their actions 'do not hold valid meetings according to the commandments' (*To the Magnesians* 4).

iii. The bishop is divinely appointed. 'Jesus Christ is by the will of the Father,' Ignatius writes to Ephesus, 'and the bishops are by the will of Jesus Christ' (*To the Ephesians* 3. 2). 'As the Lord was united to the Father, and did nothing without him, neither by himself nor through the apostles, so do you do nothing without the bishop and the presbyters' (*To the Magnesians* 17. 1).

iv. In a real sense the bishop is in the place of God and of Jesus Christ. Zotion the deacon is commended because 'he is subject to the bishop as to the grace of God, and to the presbytery as to the law of Jesus Christ' (*To the Magnesians* 2). 'We must regard the bishop as the Lord himself' (*To the Ephesians* 6. 1).

v. The only real test of an individual or a congregation is willing subjection to the bishop. Ignatius writes to the Ephesians: 'Glorify Christ by being united in subjection to the bishop and the presbytery ... It is fitting that you should live in harmony with the will of the bishop' (*To the Ephesians* 2. 2; 4. 1). He writes to the Trallians: 'When you are in subjection to the bishop as to Jesus Christ, it is clear to me that you are living not after men but after Jesus Christ ... Therefore it is necessary, as is your practice, that you should do nothing without the bishop, but also in subjection to the presbytery, as to the apostles of Jesus Christ' (*To the Trallians* 2. 1, 2). 'Submit yourself to the bishop as to the commandment, and likewise to the presbytery' (*To the Trallians* 13. 2). 'I greet her (the Church of the Philadelphians) in the blood of Jesus Christ, which is eternal and abiding joy, especially if men be at one with the bishop, and with the presbyters and deacons, who together with him have been appointed according to the mind of Jesus Christ' (*To the Philadelphians*, Preface). 'As many as belong to God and Jesus Christ, these are with the bishop' (*To the Philadelphians* 3. 2). 'Give heed to the bishop that God may give heed to you. I am devoted to those who are subject to the bishop, presbyters and deacons, and may it be mine to have my lot with them in God' (*To Polycarp* 6. 1).

Such then is the view of Ignatius. To meet the problem of disunity and of heresy he centred all things in the bishop. The bishop became the embodiment of the Church, and the very mouthpiece of the voice of God. There is as yet no dictatorship, for the bishop, the presbyters and the deacons form one whole, and the congregational meeting has its part to play, for Ignatius urges Polycarp to hold such meetings more frequently (*To Polycarp* 4. 2). But there is no doubt that with Ignatius authority is concentrated in the bishop. Unity and orthodoxy have their defence in him.

The second of the great figures in the development of authority within the Church was Irenaeus. Very little is known about his life; even his dates are uncertain. He seems to have been a native of Asia Minor, and, when he was young, he attended the lectures of Polycarp. He was born probably around A.D. 130. He knew his Greek; he could quote Homer and Hesiod, Pindar and Plato, and he knew his Bible. He became a presbyter at Lyons in Gaul. At some time while he was a presbyter he paid a visit to Rome, where Hippolytus heard him lecture. Pothinus the aged Bishop of Lyons was martyred in the savage persecution which hit the Churches of Lyons and Vienne in A.D. 177. Irenaeus was consecrated as his successor, and may well have lived until after the turn of the century.

Irenaeus lived during a time when there was a ferment

of speculation. He lived at the time when the great Gnostic systems reached their full development. He himself was a great scholar, and a meticulous investigator. Tertullian calls him 'that very exact enquirer into all doctrines' (*Against the Valentinians* 5). So Irenaeus made a careful examination and investigation of the heresies which were threatening the Church in his great book *Against Heresies*. The problem which he faced was how to know and to preserve the truth of the Christian faith.

He began from the fact that there was in fact a fixed version of the Christian faith. Ask a Christian anywhere in the world what he believes, says Irenaeus, and you will get the same answer. It does not matter if it is in the great cities, or the steppes where the nomad Scythians roam; it does not matter if the person asked is a cultured scholar or a simple soul unable even to read; it does not matter what the language spoken – in Germany, Gaul, Spain, the East, Egypt, Libya; wherever you go, whoever it be you ask, whatever the language, the answer will be the same. It is as if there was 'some precious deposit in an excellent vessel', and as if in every generation deposit and vessel alike renewed their youth (1. 10. 2; 3. 24. 1; when Irenaeus is quoted in this section, the work quoted is always *Against Heresies*).

And what is this standard version of the Christian faith? Irenaeus twice gives a summary of it, and since these summaries are long prior to the creeds they are of very great interest, and must be quoted in full. The first runs as follows:

The Church, though dispersed throughout the whole world, has received from the apostles and their disciples this faith. She believes in one God, the Father Almighty, Maker of heaven and earth and the sea, and all things that are in them; and in one Christ Jesus, the Son of God, who became incarnate for our salvation; and in the Holy Spirit who proclaimed through the prophets the dispensations of God, and the advents, and the birth from a virgin, and the passion, and the resurrection from the dead, and the ascension into heaven in the flesh of the beloved Christ Jesus our Lord, and his future manifestation from heaven in the glory of the Father, to gather all things in one, and to raise up anew all flesh of the whole human race, in order that to Christ Jesus, our Lord, and God, and Saviour, and King, according to the will of the invisible Father, every knee should bow of things in heaven and things in earth, and things under the earth, and that every tongue should confess to him, and that he should execute just judgment towards all; that he may send spiritual wickedness, and the angels who transgressed and became apostates, together with the ungodly, and unrighteous, and wicked, and profane among men, into everlasting fire; but may, in the exercise of his grace, confer immortality on the righteous, and those who have kept his commandments, and have persevered in his love, some from the beginning of their Christian course and others from the date of their repentance, and may surround them with everlasting glory (1. 10. 1).

Irenaeus says you would get the following declaration of belief amongst the barbarians who believe in Christ, 'having salvation written in their hearts by the Spirit, without paper or ink':

They believe in one God, the Creator of heaven and earth, and all things therein, by means of Christ Jesus, the Son of God; who because of his surpassing love towards his creation, condescended to be born of the virgin, he himself uniting man through himself to God, and having suffered under Pontius Pilate and rising again, and having been received up in splendour, shall come in glory, the Saviour of those who are saved, and the Judge of those who are judged, and sending into

eternal fire those who transform the truth, and despise
his Father and his advent (3. 4. 2).

Why should this common agreement exist? It exists because in the Christian Church there are successive generations of Christians who reach right back to the apostles,
and thereby to Jesus himself, for the apostles were the
companions of Jesus. T. M. Lindsay in *The Church and
the Ministry in the Early Centuries* says that the constant
argument can be summed up in the sentence: 'I knew a
man who knew a man who knew an apostle. In point of
fact Irenaeus actually says: 'I have heard from an aged
elder, who had heard it from those who had seen the
apostles, and from those who had been their disciples' (4.
27. 1).

So then Irenaeus makes his point – up and down the
world there are Churches who can trace their Christian
lineage back through the years in successive intercon-
nected generations until you get back to the apostles or to
the apostolic men and therefore ultimately to Jesus himself. So when the Church is troubled by doubts or questions or problems or uncertainties, or when it is threatened with heresies, the obvious thing to do is to go to
these men who had the best chance to know, and to ask
them what the truth is. So Irenaeus writes: 'If a dispute
about any ordinary question arises among us, should we
not have recourse to the most ancient Churches with
whom the apostles held constant intercourse, and learn
from them what is certain and clear regarding it?' (3. 4.
1).

So Irenaeus cites the case of the Roman Church. It was
founded and organised by Peter and Paul, who committed the episcopate into the hands of Linus (2 Timothy
4. 21). Anacletus succeeded him, and next came Clement
who knew the apostles and had heard them preach. Evar-
istus followed Clement, and Alexander came next. Sixtus
was the sixth in line from the apostles. Then came the

glorious martyr Telesphorus, then Pius, then Anicetus, then Soter, and finally Eleutherius, who held the Roman episcopate in Irenaeus' own day (3. 3. 3). So an apostolic succession is laid down; but it is not a succession for the transmission of grace or ministry; it is a succession for the transmission and the guarantee of truth.

Tertullian's argument is the same; the heretics cannot produce an apostolic pedigree. But Polycarp was placed in Smyrna by John, and Clement in Rome by Peter. He challenges them to run over the apostolic Churches 'in which the very thrones of the apostles are still pre-eminent in their places, in which their own authentic writings are read, uttering the voice and representing the face of each of them severally. Achaia is very near you and there you find Corinth. You are not far from Macedonia, and there you have Philippi and the Thessalonians too. Since you are able to cross to Asia, you get Ephesus. Since you are close to Italy, you have Rome' (*On Prescription against Heretics* 32; 36). As T. M. Lindsay writes: 'It is the fact of an uninterrupted succession of responsible men that is the natural and historical guarantee that the doctrines once transmitted to the fathers have been retained in the memory of the sons.'

What Irenaeus wanted to do was to take what had always been a natural Church custom and to erect it into ecclesiastical practice. He wanted to make the leaders of the Church the repositories and the guarantors of Christian truth.

It is true that Irenaeus can write: 'True knowledge is that which consists in the doctrine of the apostles, and the ancient constitution of the Church throughout all the world, and the distinctive manifestation of the body of Christ according to the successions of the bishops, by which they have handed down that Church which exists in every place, and has come even to us, being guarded and preserved, without any forging of Scriptures, by a very complete system of doctrine, and neither receiving addition nor suffering curtailment in the truth which she believes' (4. 33. 8). That passage locates the true tradition in the bishops. But more often Irenaeus locates the true tradition in the whole body of the office-bearers. He speaks of the tradition 'which originates from the apostles and which is preserved by means of the successions of elders in the Churches' (3. 2. 2). 'It behoves us,' he writes, 'to adhere to those, who, as I have already observed, do hold the doctrine of the apostles, and who together with the order of the presbyterate display sound speech and blameless conduct for the confirmation and correction of others' (4. 26. 4). He speaks of reading the Scriptures diligently 'in company with those who are the elders in the Church among whom is the apostolic doctrine, as I have pointed out' (4. 22, 1).

So two important things are to be noted about Irenaeus. He did not turn the bishop into a lonely figure, the sole repository and the ultimate dictator of truth; the truth was located not in one man but in that group of men who were the leaders of the Church. Second, Irenaeus did produce the conception of an apostolic succession; but that succession was above all things for the transmission of truth, and it was not confined to Rome – although Rome was a special case – nor to any other Church; it was the possession of every Church to whom the faith had come through the unbroken succession of its leaders.

There is one last hint in Irenaeus which is of great interest. In the early Church a *charisma* was a special gift given by God. A *charisma* was something which a man could not acquire by his own effort or diligence; it was conferred on him by the direct action of the Spirit of God. It might be the gift of preaching, of teaching, of prophesying, of healing, of administration, of speaking with tongues (1 Corinthians 12. 27–30). So Irenaeus writes: 'It is incumbent to obey the elders who are in the Church – those who, I have shown, possess the succession from the apostles; those who together with the succession of the episcopate have received *the charisma of truth* according to the good pleasure of the Father; but to hold in suspicion others who depart from the primitive succession, and assemble themselves together in any place whatsoever' (4. 26. 2). The idea is that there are certain people who have a *charisma*, a special gift from God, which enables them in their succession to receive and to transmit the truth.

With Irenaeus still more authority has been placed upon the bishop, for the bishop has become the custodian of the truth, and the arbiter of orthodoxy.

The third of the key figures in the development of authority and discipline within the Church is Cyprian – and in many ways he left the biggest effect of all.

Thascius Cyprianus, to give him his full name, was a Roman African. Of all the Church leaders he is the leader whose background most determined his policy and his point of view. He was born in Carthage about the year A.D. 200. He was a famous lawyer, a pleader and a rhetorician. He was wealthy; his gilded ceilings, his mosaics of costly marbles, his beautiful gardens were famous. He was, so to speak, a late Christian. He was baptised in the spring of A.D. 246 when he was forty-six years old. He became a presbyter in the Church of Carthage in A.D. 247. And sometime after June A.D. 248 he became bishop by popular demand. Obviously, Cyprian had a meteoric rise within the Church, and equally obviously his rise must have been others' disappointment.

From the beginning Cyprian was to show his legal training, and from the beginning he was to show that he thought of the Church in terms of the Roman Empire. A Roman provincial governor took his office from the Emperor, and he was responsible to none but the Emperor. Within the province there was no authority but his. He might consult his people, and did consult them if he was wise. It was for their good and in their interest that he

was to govern. But in authority he was answerable to
none but the Emperor and within his province he was
supreme. What may well have been his first letter shows
Cyprian's conception of his own position and of the position of the Church. According to Church law no one in
the Church's ministry could be appointed a guardian or
executor. 2 Timothy 2. 4 used the analogy of military
service: 'No soldier on service gets entangled in civilian
pursuits, since his aim is to satisfy the one who enlisted
him.' So it was held that no minister of the Church must
have anything to do with secular affairs; he must give
himself wholly and exclusively to the altar and to prayer.
A layman called Geminius Victor died having appointed
a presbyter called Geminius Faustinus – perhaps a kins-
man – guardian of his orphan children. Cyprian writes to
tell the people of Furni, where the incident happened,
that he and his colleagues were shocked, and says: 'Since
Victor ... has dared to appoint Geminius Faustinus, a
presbyter, his executor, it is not allowed that any offering
should be made by you for his repose, or any prayer be
made in Church in his name ... so that an example be
given to the rest of the brothers that no one should call
away to secular anxieties the priests and ministers of
God, who are occupied with the service of the altar and
the Church' (*Epistle* 55 (1); Cyprian's Letters are numbered differently in the Ante-Nicene Christian Library
and the Oxford Edition; in citing references we will normally give first the reference in the Ante-Nicene Christian Library, and after it in brackets the reference in the
Oxford Edition). It is easy to see how Cyprian is determined to stand by the legal rights of the Church, so determined that there is a certain element of mercilessness
in pursuing a man with penalties beyond the grave because he appointed a presbyter the guardian of his orphan children. More than a little light is shed on the
mind of Cyprian by this incident.

Cyprian enjoyed about eighteen months of a peaceful

episcopate, and then in January A.D. 250 the Decian persecution burst upon the Church. It is well to see what
that persecution was all about. The Christians not unnaturally called Decius 'an execrable animal', 'a great
snake, the pioneer of Anti-christ'. In fact Decius was an
able soldier and an upright man, fit, as one of his Latin
biographers said, to rank with the ancients. He was conscious of the weakness of the Empire and the threats
which menaced it, and he regarded the Church as a main
cause of the empire's disunity. The Romans were an essentially tolerant people. But they were searching for
some kind of principle of unity which would weld into
one the heterogeneous population of the empire, which
stretched from the Danube in the North to North Africa
in the South, and from Britain in the West to the borders
of Parthia in the East. That principle they hoped to find
in Emperor worship or Caesar worship. If a man was prepared to acknowledge the ancient gods, however form-
ally, to sacrifice to the godhead of Caesar, and to say:
'Caesar is Lord,' he could after that go away and worship
anyone he liked, so long as the worship did not conflict
with public order or public decency. In other words.
Emperor worship was far more a test of political loyalty
than it was an expression of religion, for the basic assumption behind it was that the Emperor embodied the
spirit of Rome, and that is what people were being asked
to worship. But no Christian would say 'Caesar is Lord';
for him the only possible declaration was: 'Jesus Christ is
Lord'. No Christian would take the name 'Lord' from
Jesus and give it to the Emperor or to anyone else. Therefore the Roman government saw the Christians, not so
much as religious heretics, as disaffected citizens; and
that is precisely why persecution fell with such violence
on the Christian Church.

Decius issued his edict of persecution early in A.D. 250
and the persecution raged until November of the same
year. It was worldwide; Rome, Egypt, Syria, Armenia,

Spain, North Africa all became the arenas of persecution. Death was only meant for the leaders of the Church, for Decius believed that a Church bereft of its leaders would recant. In every town and village commissioners of the sacrifices were appointed, and in the case of the ordinary Christians the aim was not to kill them, but to make them recant. So they were imprisoned, and then subjected to repeated torture, until in the end the victim either recanted or died. Those who recanted fell into three groups. There were the *sacrificati*, who sacrificed and shared in eating the sacrificial flesh and drinking the sacrificial wine. There were the *thurificati*, who burned their pinch of incense to the godhead of Caesar. In either case the sacrificer was publicly listed and he was given a *libellus*, a certificate that he had sacrificed and was known as a *libellaticus*. The standard *libellus* was worded as follows:

> To the commissioners of sacrifices of the village of Alexander's Island from Aurelius Diogenes, son of Satabus. About 72. Scar on the right eye-brow. I was both constant in always sacrificing to the gods and now in your presence according to the commands I sacrificed and drank and tasted of the victims, and I beseech you to attach your signature. May you prosper. I Aurelius Diogenes have presented this.
>   I Aurelius ... saw him sacrificing.
>   I Mystaes, son of ... have signed.
>   (These are the signatures of the magistrate and the witness).
> Dated: First year of the Emperor Caesar Gaius Messius Quintus Trajanus Decius Pius Felix Augustus. 2nd day of Ephiphi.

That particular *libellus* comes from Egypt, but the form was standard. But – and here is an important point – it was possible for a man to bribe his way to the possession of a *libellus*. If he found a corrupt official – and that was not too difficult – at a price he could buy a *libellus* without sacrificing, and so achieve safety.

If a man had been put into prison and had stood trial and had come through it, he was known as a *confessor*; if he had died or had undergone torture he was a *martyr*.

This persecution hit the Church hard. For more than a generation there had been no trouble, and the Church was soft. As H. B. Workman says in *Persecution in the Early Church*, there were 'thousands of converts who had rather changed their creeds than their characters, self-indulgent, effeminate men, painted women and ambitious clergy'. The effect was shattering. At Carthage more than half the Christians apostatised and lapsed, including even some of the clergy. At this stage Cyprian withdrew. In his essay *Concerning the Lapsed* (3) he says: 'The first title of victory is to confess the Lord after having been seized by the hands of the heathen. The second grade of glory is by a prudent retirement to save oneself for the Lord.' Cyprian was no coward; the day was to come when he was to die gloriously; but in the Decian persecution he was convinced that he could best serve God and the Church not by losing his life, but by saving it, but right though his action certainly was, it was going to make things difficult for him in the time to come.

Then the problems began. Those who had lapsed wanted to be restored to the Church; they had no desire whatever to be excluded for ever from the society and the blessings of Christianity. A Church more than half of whose members had apostatised and then wished to be restored had a major problem on its hands.

A number of factors combined to make the whole matter a very complex issue indeed. In the eyes of the Church there were certain mortal sins, and those who committed them ceased to be sons of God. Tertullian (*Concerning Modesty* 19) names as mortal sins murder, idolatry, fraud, apostasy, blasphemy, fornication, adultery. Idolatry stood high on the list, and it was idolatry which the apostates had committed, when they sacrificed to the pagan gods and to the godhead of the Emperor.

Again it was the general teaching of the Church that there was no forgiveness for post-baptismal sin. But there had come, unofficially but widely accepted, into Church thought that after baptism there was so to speak one more chance. So Hermas writes in *The Shepherd* (*Mandates* 4. 3. 6): 'But I tell you after that great and holy calling, if a man be tempted by the devil and sin, he has one repentance, but if he sin and repent repeatedly it is unprofitable for such a man, for scarcely shall he live.' But who was to say that forgiveness should be granted in such a case? This the Church would not take upon itself to do. It came to be felt that in such a case forgiveness might be granted, if there was a special revelation given by God in regard to a particular case; and, very naturally, the man to whom the revelation would normally be given was the prophet. So Tertullian writes (*Concerning Modesty* 21): 'So too had the prophets of old granted to the repentant pardon for murder and therewith adultery, inasmuch as they gave at the same time manifest proofs of severity.' This is vividly shown in the confrontation of David by Nathan the prophet. Nathan mercilessly lashed David for the murder of Uriah and the taking of Bathsheba. 'I have sinned against the Lord,' said David, and Nathan answered: 'The Lord also has put away your sin; you shall not die' (2 Samuel 12. 1–14). So even for mortal sin there could be forgiveness and restoration if a prophetic man received a revelation that it should be so.

By the time the age of persecution had arisen against the Church the prophets were nearly extinct; and the privilege of conveying forgiveness to the otherwise unforgivable sinner had descended to the martyrs. It was now open to a martyr awaiting death to issue 'letters of peace' to those who sought restoration into the Church. So Tertullian writes (*To the Martyrs* 1): 'You know that some not able to find this peace within the Church have been used to seek it from the imprisoned martyrs.' When this privilege had been used sparingly there was something infinitely moving in the picture of those who were brave enough to die beseeching pardon for those whose courage had failed. Of those waiting for martyrdom in the terrible Lyons and Vienne persecution in Gaul it is said: 'They defended all, but accused none. They absolved all, but bound none ... For they did not boast over the fallen, but helped them in their need with those things in which they themselves abounded, having the compassion of a mother, and shedding many tears on their account before the Father. They asked for life and God gave it to them and they shared it with their neighbours' (Eusebius, *The Ecclesiastical History* 5. 2. 5–7).

But things were very different in the Decian persecution. In the first place, not all the martyrs were admirable characters. There were those who were inflated with pride at their own performance. There were those who sought what they called 'the baptism of blood', for they desired what they held to be its specially redemptive qualities to give them escape from their debts, and their crimes, and their miseries. Worse, Tertullian (*Concerning Fasting* 12) hurls his contempt at the martyr Pristinus. The martyrs were kept in free custody. His devotees turned the prison into a cookshop; so far from practising abstinence he stuffed himself; he regarded the public baths as better than baptism, and the retreats of voluptuousness as more to be desired than the secrets of the Church. On the day of his trial he was so drugged with wine that he was dead drunk, so drunk that he was impervious to the scrape of the iron claws on his flesh, so intoxicated that he could answer nothing 'but hiccoughs and belchings', so bemused that he died in the very act of meaning to apostatise!

Further, the granting of these letters of peace had become nothing less than a ramp. Tertullian describes the scene in a martyr's cell: 'Adulterers beset him, fornicators gain access to him; instantly prayers echo around him; instantly pools of tears from the eyes of the polluted surround him; nor are there any more diligent in purchasing entrance to the prison than those who have lost the fellowship of the Church' (*Concerning Modesty* 22).

The letters of peace were granted quite indiscriminately, especially by the martyrs at Rome. Cyprian protested that thousands of these letters were granted daily, quite contrary to the law of the Gospel, without any distinction or enquiry into individual cases. He protested at the way in which the lapsed tried to corrupt the martyrs by fawning and flattery, by importunate and fulsome entreaties (*Epistles* 14. 2 (20. 2)).

In Rome there was a Lucian, himself a confessor, who in the name of the martyr Paulus, and in the name of a youth named Aurelius, who could not even write, issued certificates *gregatim*, in droves, and scattered them broadcast (Cyprian, *Epistles* 22. 1 (27. 1)). What could anyone do when a lapsed member turned up with a certificate from a martyr for himself *along with his friends*? In such a case, says Cyprian, thirty or more arrive in a body demanding readmission, claiming that they are kinsmen, friends, domestics – a monstrous abuse! (*Epistles* 10 (15)). When Cyprian protested direct to Lucian, who continued to issue certificates in the name of Paulus after Paulus was dead, saying that Paulus had instructed him to do so, he wrote back to Cyprian: 'Know that to all concerning whom the account of what they have done since the commission of their sin has been in your estimation satisfactory, we have granted peace; and we have desired that this rescript should be made known by you to the other bishops also. We bid you to have peace with the holy martyrs' (*Epistles* 16 (23)). In other words, anyone who applied would get a letter of peace.

It was an intolerable situation, and to a man with a mind like Cyprian's mind it was beyond bearing. Of two things Cyprian was absolutely sure. He was sure that the

Church was standing at a moment of crisis. Too easy entry into the Church had resulted in too easy apostasy, and Cyprian was quite sure that too easy restoration would at one and the same time imperil the eternal destiny of those restored and the whole future of the Church. Second, he was sure that, as the Roman Church was to put it in his support, discipline was the only rudder of the Church in the storm which had descended on her (*Epistles* 30. 2 (30)). And the situation was complicated by the fact that Cyprian was not actually at the moment with his Church, but was separated from it. Further, the acuteness of the situation was peculiar to Carthage; the clash with the martyrs and their letters of peace was a clash which happened in Carthage and nowhere else. The situation in Corinth where Dionysius was bishop was far more typical. Dionysius tells us what happened there: 'These divine martyrs among us, who now are seated with Christ, and are sharers in his kingdom, partakers of his judgment and judges with him, received some of the brothers who had fallen away and become chargeable with the guilt of sacrificing. When they perceived that their conversion and repentance were sufficient to be acceptable with him who by no means desires the death of the sinner, but his repentance, having proved them they received them back and brought them together and met with them and had fellowship with them in prayers and feasts. What counsel, brothers, do you give us concerning such persons? What should we do? Shall we have the same judgment and rule as theirs, and observe their decision and charity, and show mercy to those whom they pitied? Or shall we declare their decision unrighteous, and set ourselves as judges of their opinions, and grieve mercy and overturn order?' When Dionysius could speak to his congregation like that it is clear that the letters of peace of the martyrs in Corinth were recommendations, not dictatorial demands as they were in Carthage.

The first step in the matter came from Rome. Fabian the bishop of Rome had been one of the first to be martyred. The Church at Rome did not appoint another bishop, for, if they had done so, he too would speedily have become a martyr. They were prepared to let most things lie until the situation returned to normal; but the problem of those who had lapsed and who longed for restoration had to be dealt with at once. So the presbyters at Rome decided that those who were penitent and who were on the point of death should be restored to the fellowship of the Church (*Epistle* 51. 5 (55)). The presbyters in Carthage were in sympathy with this and would in fact have opened the door even wider, and did appear to be very leniently disposed to the lapsed. Cyprian speaks of presbyters who 'contrary to the Gospel law, ... before penance was performed, before confession even of the gravest and most heinous sin was made, before hands were placed upon the repentance by the bishops and the clergy, dare to offer on their behalf, and to give them the eucharist, that is, to profane the sacred body of the Lord, although it is written: "Whoever shall eat the bread and drink the cup of the Lord unworthily, shall be guilty of the body and blood of the Lord"' (*Epistle* 10. 1 (15)). Cyprian was rapidly finding himself at issue with his presbyters, and his problem was that he was not there to deal directly with them. There were certain things of which Cyprian was sure.

He was quite sure that open certificates from martyrs must be stopped, that if a martyr's letter of peace was granted at all, it must have the name of the lapsed person on it, so that his case could be properly investigated and a correct decision arrived at (*Epistle* 26. 2 (33)).

He was quite sure that there could be no restoration, no reception back into the communion of the Church, until confession had been made, until penance had been performed, and until the hands of *the bishop* and the clergy had been laid on the head of the man who had lapsed.

It was Cyprian's opinion that nothing should be done in a hurry, but that, when the persecution had come to an end, there should be an assembly of bishops, presbyters, deacons, confessors and representatives of the laity to decide what should be done about those who had lapsed (*Epistle* 51. 4, 5 (55)). The idea of settling the case of the lapsed by a kind of board sounds a good one, but Tertullian (*Concerning Modesty* 13) tells how the whole thing was sentimentalised, when the Roman Church gave notice that under certain conditions it would receive adulterers back: 'Why, do you yourself, when introducing into the Church, for the purpose of melting the brotherhood by his prayers, the repentant adulterer, lead him into the midst and prostrate him, all in haircloth and ashes, a compound of disgrace and horror, before the elders, suing for the tears of all, licking the footprints of all, clasping the knees of all?' Cyprian's idea of a board sounds sensible, but it too could degenerate into a maudlin charade.

Even Cyprian could see that there were cases in which consideration could not wait until the end of the storm, and even he agreed that the penitent sinner who was in the moment of death should receive restoration, and that the restoration should remain valid even if the lapsed man recovered and lived on.

Even Cyprian was sufficiently flexible to see that not all the lapsed were in the same case. He agreed that those who had succeeded in obtaining a certificate without sacrificing were not as serious sinners as those who had sacrificed, and might be received back at once. He agreed that the man who had in the end succumbed after repeated torture was not so heinous a sinner as the man who had voluntarily rushed to sacrifice to save his skin (*Epistle* 51. 13 (55)).

But Cyprian's whole problem was that he was during the persecution absent from Carthage; he, the bishop, was not there to lay his hand on the head of the accepted penitent. At first he had delegated to his presbyters, in the technical phrase, diligence and discipline. Diligence is all that is meant by pastoral care; discipline is all that has got to do with punishments and penalties. But as time went on he saw that his presbyters, or at least some of them, were out of sympathy with him. He therefore appointed an independent commission of five to look after discipline, and that action not unnaturally split the Church in Carthage.

In due time Cyprian came back to Carthage, and such was the force of his personality that he got his own way in the end. And this victory of Cyprian marks a very important stage in the development of authority within the Church. Cyprian was adamant on two things.

First, he was adamant on the place of the Church. It was Cyprian who said: 'He can no longer have God for his Father, who has not the Church for his mother' (*On the Unity of the Church* 6), which comes very near to Augustine's yet more famous: '*Extra ecclesiam nulla salus*. There is no salvation outside the Church' (Augustine, *Concerning Baptism* 4. 17, 24). Cyprian had no idea of an invisible Church. To him the Church was the Church which you can see, the one Catholic Church. He precedes the saying we have just quoted with the words: 'He who forsakes the Church of Christ cannot attain to the rewards of Christ. He is a stranger; he is profane; he is an enemy.' And at the end of the same chapter he writes: 'He who does not hold this unity does not hold God's law, does not hold the faith of the Father and the Son, does not hold life and salvation.' In another place he writes: 'Whoever he may be, and whatever he may be, he who is not in the Church of Christ is not a Christian' *Epistle* 51. 24 (55)).

Second, to Cyprian there was a corollary to this – the Church centred in the bishop. No one ever had a higher idea of the office of a bishop than Cyprian had. 'The bishop is in the Church, and the Church is in the bishop, and, if anyone is not with the bishop, he is not in the Church' (*Epistle* 68. 8 (66)). 'Our Lord, whose precepts and admonitions we ought to observe, describing the honour of a bishop and the order of his Church, speaks in the Gospel and says to Peter: "I say to you, You are Peter, and on this rock I will build my Church; and the gates of hell will not prevail against it. And I will give you the keys of the kingdom of heaven; and whatever you shall bind on earth shall be bound in heaven; and whatever you loose on earth shall be loosed in heaven." Thence, through the changes of times and successions, the ordering of bishops and the plan of the Church flows onward; so that the Church is founded on the bishops, and every act of the Church is controlled by these same rulers' (*Epistle* 26. 1 (33)). Epistle 54 (59) has much to say about the bishop. He has the sublime power of government in the Church. Scripture lays it down that he who is disobedient to the priest is to be slain (Deuteronomy 17. 12, 13). Heresies and schisms arise when the priest is disobeyed. The bishop is judge in the stead of Christ. To judge the bishop is to judge God. Christ appoints and protects his priests. If God is concerned with the fall of the sparrow on the ground, how much more must he be concerned with the appointment of the bishops who are his stewards? (*Epistle* 54 (59) 4, 5, 6). In one passage (*Epistle* 68. 5 (66)) a whole series of great titles are given to the bishop – the overseer of the brotherhood, the provost of the people, the pastor of the flock, the governor of the Church, the representative of Christ, the priest of God.

T. M. Lindsay in *The Church and the Ministry in the Early Centuries* collects the various references to the bishop's connection with discipline. The bishop is in entire charge of the discipline of the congregation and it is his duty to instruct the congregation in the discipline which the Church according to the Scriptures requires from the people (61. 2 (4); 5. 2 (14); 10. 2 (15); 9. 3

(16)). The elders and the deacons, the confessors and the martyrs may assist him, but always under his control. 'Those who so devotedly and bravely maintain the faith of the Lord should maintain the law and discipline of the Lord' (10. 1 (15); 11. 2 (17); 12 (18); 13 (19)). To the bishop alone there belongs the right of binding and losing, originally given to Peter, and then descending to all the bishops (72. 7 (23)). The restoration of sinners is never possible until the bishop has heard their confessions, prescribed, and approved of, their signs of sorrow, and with the elders and deacons has placed his hands on their head in token of forgiveness (9. 2 (16); 13 (18); 14. 3 (20); 53 (57); 9. 2 (16)). 'We,' writes Cyprian, 'by whom account is to be given to the Lord, are anxiously weighing and carefully examining who ought to be received and admitted into the Church' (54. 15 (59)).

It would hardly be stretching the truth to say that the sinner was at the mercy of the Church, and in particular at the mercy of the bishop. It was Cyprian's claim that it was the exclusive right of the bishop to grant absolution to the sinner. Cyprian is well aware, and can say, that God alone can forgive sin. The Church can do no more than convey the forgiveness of God to the sinner and pronounce absolution for him. But there are times when Cyprian speaks as if the Church and the bishop had the right actually to forgive, not in their own power, but acting as the representatives of God. As it has been not unfairly put, Cyprian does give the impression of identifying Church absolution and divine pardon.

With Cyprian the authority of the Church over its members became more absolute than ever it had been before, and its discipline became more rigorous and severe.

Before we leave the days of the Fathers of the Church we shall look at two more of them.

First, we shall look at an incident which shows just how absolute the authority of the Church was. Ambrose was bishop of Milan from A.D. 374 to 397, and he was one of the greatest bishops the Church ever had. During part of that time Theodosius was emperor. Theodosius was a convinced and devoted Christian, but he had an explosive temper which lead him into actions which afterwards he was to regret. Thessalonica was a city which Theodosius knew well, for he had lived and been baptised there. In the year A.D. 390 Botherich was governor of Thessalonica, an upright and honourable man. Botherich committed to prison a depraved charioteer, who was a popular hero. The people demanded the release of the charioteer, and Botherich rightly refused. Thereupon the people rioted and murdered Botherich and other magistrates, and dragged their bodies through the streets. Theodosius was enraged. For a time he was prevailed on to take things calmly, but his courtiers and especially his chief minister Rufinus, his evil genius, inflamed his passion, and an avenging force was despatched to Thessalonica. Theodosius repented of his wrath and changed his mind. But it was too late; there was no way of speedy communication in those days and the order cancelling the vengeance did not arrive in time. It was the day of a great race in Thessalonica and the circus was packed to the limit. The gates were closed so that none could escape. The soldiers were unleashed on the crowd. For three hours they slaughtered, young and old, innocent and guilty, and at least seven thousand people perished.

When the news reached the West there was a shudder of horror. When Ambrose knew that Theodosius was on his way to Milan, he temporarily absented himself from the city. He wrote a letter to Theodosius, commanding him to repent and warning him that he would not be allowed into the cathedral. He hoped that by giving this breathing space he might make it possible for Theodosius to repent. When Sunday came Ambrose had returned and Theodosius presented himself at the cathedral. Theodosius was the Emperor of Rome, the most powerful man in the world, but Ambrose the bishop halted him in his tracks. He barred him from the cathedral. 'With what eyes,' he said to him, 'will you look on the temple of our common Lord? With what feet will you tread that holy threshold? How will you stretch forth your hands still dripping with the blood of unjust slaughter? How in such hands will you receive the all holy Body of the Lord? How will you who in your rage unrighteously poured forth so much blood lift to your lips the precious blood? Begone! Do not attempt to add another crime to that which you have committed. Submit to the restriction to which God the Lord of all agrees that you be sentenced. He will be your physician, he will give you health.' And Theodosius turned away.

Theodosius was broken-hearted for he truly loved the Church and the Church's Lord. For eight months he mourned. Rufinus came upon the Emperor in tears and smiled cynically. 'You smile,' said Theodosius, 'because you do not know my misery. The Church of God is open to slaves and beggars; it is closed to me, and with it the gates of heaven,' for Theodosius knew and accepted the saying about binding and loosing being in the bishop's power.

Rufinus offered to go to Ambrose and plead his case, and told Theodosius to follow. Ambrose was adamant; until Theodosius did fitting penance the doors were closed. By this time Theodosius was on the way and had reached the middle of the forum. Rufinus sent him word that Ambrose would not admit him, but Theodosius would not turn back. 'I will go,' he said, 'and accept the disgrace I deserve.'

So Theodosius arrived pleading for entrance to the Church. 'What repentance have you shown?' Ambrose demanded. Theodosius humbly asked what he must do. Ambrose laid down two conditions. First, Theodosius must make a law that thirty days were to elapse between the passing of a verdict and the carrying of it out, so that no sudden volcanic moment of passion could wreck things again. Theodosius agreed. Second, Ambrose insisted that Theodosius should take his place among the ordinary penitents. So the Emperor of Rome came to the cathedral door, and lay prostrate on the ground. As Theodoret the ancient historian writes: 'He plucked out his hair; he smote his head; he besprinkled the ground with the drops of his tears and prayed for pardon.' Thus the Emperor of Rome had to humble himself in penitence before the Church's doors and holy table were open to him again.

There came after his restoration a day when Theodosius brought his offering to the chancel steps. Not of set purpose, but without thinking, he remained within the sanctuary after he had given his offering. Ambrose sent him orders to get back among the congregation and not to trespass on that part of the Church which was open only to the priests. 'Purple, sir,' he said, 'can make an emperor, but not a priest.' And Theodosius stepped down and gave grateful thanks for the warning.

Such was the authority of the Church. In the days of Ambrose the Emperor of the world had to abase himself before it.

Last of the great patristic figures to appear in the development of the idea of authority within the Church is Augustine. Augustine was Bishop of Hippo in North Africa from A.D. 395 to 430. No one would deny that Augustine is one of the supreme figures of the Christian Church, but in the matter of authority Augustine was responsible for some of the most terrible crimes which have disfigured the history of the Church.

In the Parable of the Great Feast in Luke 14. 15–24 Jesus told the story of the man who prepared a great banquet only to find that all the invited guests made excuses for not coming to the feast. The servants were then sent out to the streets and the lanes, the highways and the hedges, to bring in the poor, the maimed, the blind and

the lame. As Luke tells the story, the final instruction of
the giver of the feast to his servants in his search for
guests is: 'Go out to the highways and the hedges, *and
compel people to come in*, that my house may be filled'
(Luke 14. 23). 'Compel people to come in' – Augustine
tore these words from their context, and used them to
claim that it was right *to compel* people to come into the
Church, to exercise force to coerce them into becoming
Christian, to use torture and even death to force people
to become Christians.

Even the great pagans had laid down the principle of
religious liberty. Julian, the Emperor who had tried to
put the clock back and to bring back the old gods, had
said: 'Neither fire nor sword can change the fate of mankind; the heart disowns the hand which is compelled by
terror to sacrifice, and persecution only makes hypocrites
and martyrs' (*Epistle* 7). Saying after saying can be cited
from Christian writers insisting on the sanctity of religious liberty. Tertullian said: 'It is a fundamental
human right, a privilege of nature, that every man
should worship according to his own convictions; one
man's religion neither harms nor helps another man. It is
assuredly no part of religion to compel religion, to which
free-will and not force should lead us, the sacrificial victims being required of a willing mind' (*To Scapula* 2).
'Let one man worship God, another Jupiter. Let one man
lift suppliant hands to the heavens, another to the altar
of Fides. Let one – if you choose to take this view of it –
count in prayer the clouds, and another the panels of the
ceiling. Let one consecrate his own life to God, and another that of a goat. For see that you do not give a further
ground for the charge of irreligion by taking away religious liberty, and forbidding free choice of deity, so that
I may no longer worship according to my inclination, but
am compelled to worship against it. Not even a human
being would care to have an unwilling homage rendered
to him' (*Apology* 24). Lactantius writes: 'Religion is

alone the seat in which Liberty has placed her home. It is a thing which. beyond all else, is voluntary, nor can necessity be imposed on anyone to worship what he does not wish. A man may perhaps pretend, he cannot will, to do it' (*Epitome* 24). 'There is no need of violence and injury, for religion cannot be imposed by force. It is by words (*verbis*) rather than by blows (*verberibus*) that the matter must be carried on, in order that it may be a matter of voluntary choice ... It is not in killing but in dying that religion must find its defence; not in savagery but in patient endurance; not in crime but in fidelity. If you wish to defend religion by bloodshed and tortures and injury, it is not defended; it is violated and polluted. Nothing is so much a matter of free-will as religion, for, if in matters of religion the mind of the worshipper is opposed to the worship, then religion is destroyed and is no religion at all' (*The Institutes* 5. 20). Athanasius said: Nothing more forcibly marks the weakness of a bad cause then persecution' (*History of the Arians* 4. 7). 'Satan, because there is no truth in him, breaks in with axe and sword. But the Saviour is gentle, and forces no one to whom he comes, but knocks and speaks to the soul: "Open to me, my sister"' (*Song of Solomon* 5. 2).

There was a time when Augustine himself would have agreed with this. In a sermon on John (*Sermon* 26. 2) he writes: 'If we are dragged to Christ, we believe against our will; violence is applied; the will is not kindled. A man may enter the church against his will; he may receive the sacrament against his will; but he cannot believe against his will ... Since he who is dragged seems to be compelled against this will, how do we solve the question: "No man comes to me except my Father draws him"?' There was a time when Augustine could say that he believed that: 'Truth alone wins the victory, and the victory of truth is love.' But in his *Retractions* he tells how he changed his mind. 'My original opinion,' he said, 'was that no one ought to be coerced into Christian unity, that the matter should be carried on by word, that the battle should be by argument, that the victory should be won by reason, lest we should have people becoming apparent members of the Catholic Church whom we had previously known to be open heretics. But this opinion of mine was overcome, not by the words of those who argued against it, but by the example of those who demonstrated it to be wrong.' He had, he said, withdrawn his opinion that schismatics should not be brought into the communion of the Church by the use of the force and the attack of the secular power, because of the sheer badness of the heretics, and because of the proved effectiveness of 'the diligence of discipline'.

Augustine defended his view by saying: 'We must not consider *that* one is compelled; we must consider *what* it is to which he is compelled' (*Epistle* 93. 16). He argued that there was no real invasion of the rights of conscience; in fact the freedom of conscience was being preserved by the removal of obstacles from the progress of the truth. Cruelty, as it has been put, was disguised as mercy, on the grounds that it was inflicted in the eternal interests of the persecuted. F. W. Farrar summed up in three steps the way in which Augustine's mind worked. First, he began with the principle: 'Outside the Church there is no salvation.' Second, he went on to argue, in effect: 'There is no Church but mine. Mine is the Church outside which there is no salvation.' Thirdly, he then reached the conclusion: 'It is, therefore, to your interest, that I should force you into membership of the Church by making you accept my convictions whether you hold them or not, if need be by reducing you to destitution, driving you into exile or putting you to death, if you refuse.' It was precisely the misuse of this phrase from a parable, this false argument that it was all being done in the interest of the person coerced, which, as Farrar says, produced 'the Albigensian crusades, Spanish armadas, Netherlands butcheries, St. Bartholomew mas-

sacres, the accursed infamies of the Inquisition, the vile
espionage, the hideous balefires of Seville and Smithfield,
the racks, the gibbets, the thumbscrews, the subterranean
torture-chambers used by churchly torturers who assumed
the garb and language of priests with the trade and
temper of executioners'. It was a bad day for the Church,
when Augustine with perverted ingenuity misinterpreted
a chance phrase of Scripture to suit the misguided purposes of the Church.

So it happens that there emerges on the scene a man
with an' odd distinction – the first heretic to be executed
for his heresy. His name was Priscillian, and along with
four followers, Felicissimus, Armenius, the poet Latro-
nianus, and the wealthy widow Euchrotia, he was be-
headed in A.D. 385. He was Bishop of Avila in Spain. He
was a kind of latter day Gnostic. He accepted as sacred
books outside the canon. The body for him was evil.
Angels and human souls were emanations from God. The
soul was united to the body in punishment for sin. The
Devil was not a fallen angel; he was the principle of evil,
and the creator of the body. Priscillian naturally held
docetic, seemist, views of Jesus, holding him to have no
real body, but to be only a phantom in human shape.
Marriage and the begetting of children were forbidden,
although free love was allowed. Priscillian and his friends
were vegetarians and refused to eat flesh of any kind. He
and his friends were executed on the charge of sorcery
and immorality. Priscillian acquired a good many followers and the Priscillianists lingered on until the sixth
century.

For the most part the Church was shocked with the
whole proceeding. Both Ambrose and Pope Damasus of
Rome refused to communicate with the Spanish bishops
who were responsible for Priscillian's execution. Martin of
Tours insisted: 'Let us have no bloodshed in matters of
religion.' As the historian Sulpicius Severus tells us (2. 50)
Martin maintained that 'it was quite sufficient punish-

ment that, having been declared heretics by a sentence of the bishops, they should have been expelled from the Churches; and that it was besides a foul and unheard of indignity that a secular ruler should be judge in an ecclesiastical cause'. Priscillian was only the first of a long line of heretics whom the Church was to torture and slay allegedly for their own good.

By the fifth century the Church had developed a very absolute authority, an authority which claimed to shut against a man, not only the doors of the Church on earth, but also the gates of the Kingdom of Heaven, and an authority which was more and more backed by the power of the state.

Chapter 6

Authority in the Church
In Mediaeval and Reformation Times

Even in patristic times, which we have just been considering, the treatment of the penitent sinner by the authority
of the Church was becoming more and more systematised.
The length of penance which the penitent sinner must
undertake was made proportionate to the seriousness
of his sin. So the various Church Councils lay down
the period of penance – for the lapsed, anything from
two to thirteen years; for adultery, seven years; for
women who used prepared drugs to bring about abor-
tions, ten years; for a wilful murderer, life; for an in-
voluntary homicide, five years; for diviners, sorcerers or
astrologers, five years; for seduction, ten years; for idolatry, life; for extravagant dress, three years; for gambling,
one year. The penance would involve prayer and fasting
and sexual continence and exclusion from the Lord's
Supper.

Nor was the way back easy. The penitents went
through certain stages. They began by being *prosklai-
ontes* in Greek, *flentes* in Latin, that is, weepers. At this
stage they had to stand in the courtyard before the
Church door, when the congregation was assembling for
worship, weeping and beseeching those who were entering the Church to pity them and to support their plea for
restoration. At the second stage, the penitents were *ak-
roōmenoi,* or *audientes,* that is, hearers. At this stage they
were allowed to be present in a distant part of the

Church, and to hear the reading of Scripture and the preaching of the sermon. At the third stage, the penitents were *hupopiptontes*, or *prostrati*, that is, kneclers. At this stage, they were allowed to take part in those items of the service in which the catechumens shared, kneeling for prayer. At the fourth and last stage, the penitents were *sunistamenoi*, or *consistentes*, that is, standers. At this stage they were allowed to look on standing while the Eucharist was being celebrated, although they were not allowed to participate. Then came the final restoration, the laying on of hands by the bishop, the kiss of peace, and admission to the Table of the Lord. The way back for the penitent sinner was never an easy way.

Bit by bit the act of penance became more and more elaborate and more and more important, until it became not merely an act and a system, but a sacrament. It was Gregory the Great who systematised penance and gave it the form in which it was established in the Middle Ages. In this systematisation there were five elements: i. It began with the perception and the realisation of sin; ii. This moved the penitent to the fear of the judgment of God. These two initial stages were known as the *conversio mentis*, the conversion of the mind; iii. Next there came regret, contrition, *contritio*, sorrow for sin; iv. This was followed by confession of sin to the priest; v. And lastly, there came satisfaction, the carrying out of the things laid down as necessary by the priest. Two things have to be noted.

First, increasingly satisfaction became the principal thing. Harnack defines satisfaction as 'the necessary manifestation of sorrow through works that are fitted to furnish a certain satisfaction to the injured God'. We need to be careful to understand this rightly and fairly. There never was any question of a man working his passage, paying his way, earning his release. At all times the merit of Jesus Christ and his sacrifice is the one essential thing. But Harnack identifies three reasons why satisfaction was demanded. First, a man *can* render a certain satisfaction; he can by his own effort cooperate with the all-availing sacrifice of Jesus Christ; he can do something to show to God that his sorrow is real. Second, if a man passes through the discipline and the rigour of penance, he is bound to emerge from it a better man. Third, the very fact that he has undertaken and undergone this penance is bound to protect him from further sins. Further, it is of primary importance to remember that the satisfaction in question is not valid unless the offerer of it is already in a state of grace. He must first be absolved and then he must offer the satisfaction which he promised before his absolution.

Second, penance became the most important sacrament in the Church. At baptism a man's previous sins are all forgiven; but a man can only be baptised once. And just because we are human beings life is continually polluted and stained; it cannot be otherwise. So penance becomes 'the baptism of tears'. It becomes what Tertullian called 'the second plank after shipwreck'. Baptism can only happen once; but the sacrament of penance can be repeatedly administered. And surely every baptised person needs it. Penance therefore became the most important means of grace. The Church, as Harnack put it, becomes saturated with this sacrament. Two things are to be said.

First, if there could be such a thing as perfect contrition, then there would be no need of any further satisfaction. But it is not in man to bring to God this perfect contrition, and the sacrament comes to be not far off from being a substitute for contrition. Second, clearly, the more fundamental the sacrament of penance becomes, the greater the power of the priest. True, only God forgives sin, but there is a sense in which the priests are his 'authorised ministers'. Thomas Aquinas has it: 'The salvation of the sinner – that is, that his sin be removed from him – is not possible without the sacrament of penance, in which there operates the virtue of Christ's passion, through absolution of the priest together with the work of the penitent, who cooperates with grace for the destruction of sin.'

It is plain to see with what authority all this clothed the Church. As Harnack put it, 'the Church became the indispensable preliminary condition to salvation ... The Church alone saves from damnation.' Trust in God's grace became weaker and trust in the Church became stronger. The Church becomes 'the indispensable medium to guarantee the possibility of salvation'. The sacrament of penance placed the very authority of salvation in the hands of the Church. The Church became the custodian of a man's eternal destiny.

The other great development within the period preceding the Reformation was the development in what might be called the aggressiveness of the Church's attitude towards the heretic and those who opposed it, and the increasing insistence that the secular power existed to carry out the decisions of the spiritual power. In other words, the Church was demanding and in many cases receiving an ever greater authority, not only within its own sphere, but also within the sphere of the state.

This process had its beginning in the early part of the fourth century when Christianity under Constantine became the approved religion of the Roman Empire. A situation arose in which the Emperor could define and proceed against heretics, and in which the state exercised disciplinary measures against the heretic, by confiscation of his goods, banishment, fines, imprisonment and even death. The great Theodosian code of laws (A.D. 438) laid it down that every offence against religion was a public crime, because such offences – by offending God – brought injury to all. The Nicene creed was taken as the standard, and those who would not accept it were liable to be deprived of all religious rights, to be excluded from all civil office, and to be liable to all the penalties of the law. The code of Justinian (A.D. 534), which may be said to have finalised Roman law, made regulations for all kinds of ecclesiastical affairs. And since it was based on the principle that in all things the will of the monarch is supreme, it gave the monarch control even of ecclesiastical affairs.

The authority of the Church was becoming greater and wider, and its connection with the state closer and closer. The Pope claimed to be, and was accepted as, the Vicar of Christ; he was therefore the supreme exerciser of authority and of discipline. He could impose sentence of anathema, which in the case of an individual shut out the person from the Lord's Table and from all public services of the Church except preaching; and, if the anathema was in force when the person died, he could not be buried in consecrated ground. If the anathema was pronounced on a territory, the sacraments could not be dispensed, the administration of the Eucharist, of ordination and of supreme unction were forbidden, all public services of the Church were banned, and no one might be buried in consecrated ground. The comprehensiveness of an anathema can be seen in the anathema which was pronounced by Pope Clement the Sixth on Louis the Bavarian: 'Let him be damned in his going out and his coming in! The Lord strike him with madness and blindness and mental insanity! May the heavens empty upon him thunderbolts, and the wrath of the Omnipotent burn itself into him in the present and the future world! May the universe fight against him and the earth open to swallow him alive!' The Church is now claiming the authority to damn a man to all eternity.

It is possible to trace the claims of the Church to authority through a succession of events. At the Synod of Toulouse in A.D. 1163 heretics were said to be like snakes concealing themselves in the grass and princes were called upon to take an oath to obliterate them. At the Twelfth Ecumenical Council of A.D. 1215 Innocent the Third established the tribunal of the Inquisition 'to meet

the peril of heresy and to extirpate it'. At the Fourth
Lateran Council in A.D. 1215 princes were again enjoined
to proceed against heretics, and to those who did so the
same indulgences were promised as to those who took
part in the Crusades to regain the Holy Sepulchre. At the
Council of Toulouse in A.D. 1229 torture was prescribed
as a means of extracting confession from heretics. No
heretic was to be punished until he was found guilty by
an ecclesiastical court, but once such a court did find him
guilty, the secular power was bound to take action to
destroy his home, confiscate his goods and put him to
death. Blasphemy against God and the Son of God was a
worse crime than treason. The Church did not itself execute the condemned, but any prince who refused to do
so was threatened with exclusion not only from the sacrament but also from heaven.

The burning of heretics became an accepted principle.
Bernard Guy said: 'Heretics can only be exterminated as
heretics are burned.' The Schoolmen took the same view.
Thomas Aquinas wrote: 'Heretics are to be separated,
not only from the Church by excommunication, but also
from the world by death.' 'As falsifiers of coin are to be
put to death, much more should they be put to death
who are guilty of the more wicked act of corrupting the
faith. The Church delivers the heretic to the secular tribunal to be put out of the world.' It was in 1478 that
Sixtus the Fourth approved the setting up of the Spanish
Inquisition, which brought to a fine, if diabolical art, the
practice of torture to compel the heretic to recant.

Finally, on 18th November 1302 Boniface the Eighth
issued the papal bull *unam sanctam* which has been
called 'the zenith of mediaeval papal ecclesiastical pol-
ity.' The background of the bull was Boniface's quarrel
with Philip the Fourth of France. It was set down that
there was one holy catholic apostolic Church, outside of
which there is neither salvation nor remission of sins. Of
that Church the Pope is the supreme head, and to reject

the authority of the Pope is to cease to belong to the Church. Both swords, the temporal and the spiritual swords, are committed to the Church. The spiritual sword is of course in the hands of the clergy. The temporal sword is delegated to the secular authority, but it is to be used on the Church's behalf, and under the Church's direction. The spiritual is always greater than the temporal. Therefore the temporal power must always be subordinate to the spiritual power. The spiritual power itself is subject to nothing other than the judgment of God himself. The spiritual power was granted by God himself to Peter and his successors. It therefore follows that to oppose the spiritual power is to do nothing other than to oppose God. It is therefore necessary for salvation for every human being to be subject to the Roman Pope. There cannot be a more comprehensive claim to authority than that.

So then as the Church approached the time of the Reformation its claim to authority is absolute over a man in this life, and its authority is such that it can settle a man's entry to heaven, and can open or shut to men the gateway to the presence of God. In truth at that time the Church had reached the zenith of its claim to authority.

Just as the Church of the patristic days had its hour of supreme. triumph in the Ambrose confrontation with Theodosius, so the mediaeval Church had its most spectacular hour in the humiliation of Henry the Second after the murder of Thomas Becket. Becket was murdered in his own cathedral of Canterbury on 29th December 1170, and, however much he might afterwards deny it, Henry the Second was responsible for the murder. In 1174 Henry the Second set sail from France to England, and a troubled and rebellious country at that time England was. He landed at Southampton and straight away set out for Canterbury, subsisting on a diet of bread and water. He travelled the last stage of the journey clad in the hair shirt and the woollen shift of a pilgrim. He arrived in Canterbury on 12th July 1174. From St. Dunstan's Church he walked to the Cathedral barefoot in the rain. He kissed the stone of martyrdom; he knelt and wept and prayed at Becket's tomb. He declared his penitence; he promised grants by which the lights on Becket's tomb would burn for ever; and then the king of England lay on the ground and submitted to be flogged by the bishops, the abbot and each of the eighty monks, and he spent the night alone in the crypt in fasting and in prayer. Once again the Church had shown its authority. At the Church's bidding the king of England submitted to being scourged.

So the Reformation came, and at the Reformation the reformed Church did not lower its claims to authority and to discipline, but there was a difference. There were four basic differences in the attitude of the Protestant Church: i. The Protestant Church introduced the principle of each man's immediate responsibility to God, without the intervention of any priesthood; ii. The Protestant Church took as the supreme rule of faith and life the Scriptures, and the Scriptures in the people's own tongue. The last word was no longer with the Pope; it was with the Bible; iii. The Protestant Church laid a very great stress on preaching. Preaching, instruction, persuasion were meant to replace penal discipline; iv. The confessional was abolished, and inward repentance of the heart took the place of penance with its system of satisfactions dictated by the priest. Within the Protestant Church authority and discipline were going to be different, but none the less they were still going to be very real.

First, let us look at authority and discipline as John Calvin saw them. Calvin was by nature and character and ability a great administrator. He formed a group of twelve elders, and set them to live in different parts of Geneva to carry out their duty of oversight. They had to watch over the religious and moral welfare of the people. They were obliged to visit each home at least once a year.

They formed the consistory along with the pastors. They dealt with complaints against anyone, no matter who he was. They dealt themselves with lesser offences, like not attending Church. The more serious offenders were handed over to the civil authorities. Calvin regarded the state as a divinely appointed institution intended to defend the Church and to punish religious as well as political and moral offences. Sedition, adultery, blasphemy, idolatry, heresy were all punishable by death – and Scriptural warrant was found for such a punishment. So Servetus was burned on the charges of blasphemy and of rejecting infant baptism – and Calvin himself acted as prosecutor. But Calvin insisted that excommunication was the prerogative of the Church and of the Church alone, and declared that he would die rather than allow the state to interfere in this.

Calvin's considered views of Church authority and Church discipline are set out in the twelfth chapter of the fourth book of the *Institutes*. There are some, he says, who hate the very word discipline. But there is no society, no house, no family, which can be kept in a right state without discipline. How much more the Church? Discipline is a curb to restrain and tame those who war against the doctrine of Christ; it is a stimulus by which the indifferent are aroused; it is a fatherly rod by which those who have erred are chastised in mercy.

It is a first duty to proceed by private admonition, especially in cases of mere delinquencies; but when it is a matter of open and flagrant sin, when it is a matter of the adulterer, the fornicator, the thief, the robber, the seditious, the perjurer, the false witness, the contumacious, then something more than admonition is necessary; there must be banishment from the Christian fellowship.

In admonition and correction, even in excommunication, in all Christian discipline, there are three aims. First, God is not to be insulted by the giving of the name Christian to those who live shameful and flagitious lives, as if his holy Church was an assembly of the wicked and the abandoned. There must be nothing in the Church to bring disgrace on the sacred name. As for the Lord's Supper, it is as great a sacrilege to admit to it an unworthy person as to have thrown the Lord's body to dogs. Second, there must be discipline, so that the good — as can so easily happen — may not be corrupted by constant communication with the wicked. There is such a thing as the seduction of a bad example. Third, it is to the interest of the sinner to be chastised, so that he may be ashamed and may begin to repent of his turpitude. To show him indulgence would only make him more obstinate in sin; the rod may rouse him to penitence; and temporal punishment may save a man from eternal punishment.

In mere delinquencies, in lighter offences, there is no occasion for undue severity. Verbal chastisement is sufficient, and chastisement given in a gentle and a fatherly way, so as not to exasperate or confound the offender, but to bring him back to himself, so that he may end by rejoicing and not grieving at the correction. But in serious fault this is not enough. In such a case the person in fault should be denied the communion of the Lord's Supper at least for a time. He must be restored by the laying on of hands. The consent of the people must be given and the ceremony of restoration must be made as impressive as possible. No one, not even kings, are to be exempt. Kings who are surrounded by flattery should be grateful for the honesty of the church. There should be over the whole proceeding a gravity bespeaking the presence of Christ, and leaving no doubt that he is presiding over his own tribunal.

Yet withal discipline is to be exercised in the spirit of meekness, for the object of it is always to bring the sinner to repentance. Calvin looks back on the early days when discipline lasted for three, for four, for seven years, for life. 'What could this cause but either great hypocrisy or very great despair?' Calvin will not have it that there is

no second repentance – it is not reasonable. He quotes
Chrysostom; 'If God is so kind, why should his priests
wish to appear austere?' Discipline should be exercised
not with rigour but with charity. Leave it to God to condemn. 'Whenever it seems good to him, the worst are
changed into the best.' It is true that the right to bind
and to loose is given to the Church. But this means censure. It does not, and cannot, mean that the Church can
consign anyone to perpetual ruin and damnation. It can
only warn him of what must follow if he does not repent.
Excommunication rebukes and punishes and warns; but
only in order ultimately to bring salvation; reconcilia-
tion and restoration are waiting to be given. We are not
to count a man an enemy, but to admonish him as a
brother. Discipline must never 'degenerate into destruction'.

Calvin quotes Augustine in his earlier days; church
discipline ought always to have regard to the unity of the
Spirit in the bond of peace. Unless we remember this, the
medicine of discipline ceases to be a medicine and becomes a pernicious thing. Intemperate correction can
burst the bonds of society. At all costs schism is to be
avoided. Correction is to be carried out 'without impair-
ing the sincerity of love or breaking the bond of peace'.
Discipline is not to be perverted to 'sacrilegious schism
and purposes of excision'. Especially when the contagion
is widespread, mercy and discipline must go hand in
hand. Calvin quotes Augustine's wish to do something
about the drunkenness prevalent in North Africa: 'In
my opinion, such doings are not removed by rough, harsh
and imperious measures, but more by teaching than commanding, more by admonishing than threatening. For it
is thus we ought to act with a multitude of offenders.
Severity is to be exercised against the sins of the few.'
Correction is to be aimed to give 'soundness to the body
rather than destruction'.

Calvin will not relax discipline, but the whole tone of

his conception of discipline is that discipline is always to be exercised with the one aim of the restoration of the sinner and the preservation of the unity of the Church.

We now turn to John Knox. In his *Liturgy* Knox has a section on Ecclesiastical Discipline and an Order of Excommunication and of Public Repentance. In his section on Ecclesiastical Discipline he is clearly indebted to Calvin. No city, town, house or family, he says, can maintain its estate without 'policy and government'. This is still truer of the Church, for in the nature of things the Church must be purer than any other institution. The word of God is the life and soul of the Church; godly order and discipline are the sinews of the body, which join the members together in 'decent order and comeliness'.

'Discipline is a bridle to stay the wicked from their mischief. It is a spur to prick forward such as are slow and negligent; yea, and for all men it is the Father's rod, ever in readiness to chastise gently the faults committed, and to cause them afterward to live in more godly fear and reverence. Finally, it is an order left by God unto his Church, whereby men learn to frame their wills and doings according to the law of God, by instructing and admonishing one another, yea, and by correcting and punishing all obstinate rebels and contemners of the same.'

Like Calvin, Knox sets down the three reasons for discipline. First, discipline is necessary in order that men of evil conduct may not be numbered amongst God's children to their Father's reproach, as if the Church were 'a sanctuary for naughty and vile persons'. Second, discipline is necessary in order that the good may not be infected by companying with the evil, for there is always the risk that a little leaven will leaven the whole lump. Thirdly, discipline is necessary in order that the man who is corrected or excommunicated may be ashamed of his fault, and so repent and be amended.

Discipline can be public or private, but, whichever it

is, the aim must ever be to win and not to slander. Those who exercise discipline must make sure that the fault is 'reprovable by God's word'. And always 'modesty and wisdom' must be used that the man may come to see and realise his own fault.

Nothing deserving of discipline is to be passed over without some punishment – 'anything evil in example, slanderous in manner, not becoming their profession; any covetous person, any adulterer or fornicator, forsworn, thief, briber, false witness-bearer, blasphemer, drunkard, slanderer, usurer; any person disobedient, seditious or dissolute; any heresy or sect, as Papistical, Anabaptistical, and such like; briefly, whatsoever it be that might spot the Christian congregation, yea, rather whatsoever is not to edification, ought not to escape either admonition or punishment.'

Excommunication is 'the apostolical rod and correction'. And since it is 'the greatest and last punishment' belonging to the spiritual ministry, it should never be imposed without the decision of the whole Church. Care must always be taken to be more ready to receive than to expel. Even if a man is excluded from the sacrament, he must still be permitted to hear the sermon, so that he may have every opportunity to become penitent. That which God's word ordains and allows must never be exceeded – and always applied with mercy.

John Knox has in his *Liturgy* an Order of Excommunication and of Public Repentance. He begins by saying that all crimes which by the law of God deserve death also deserve excommunication, and he goes on to list 'wilful murderers, lawfully convicted adulterers, sorcerers, witches, conjurers, charmers, givers of drinks to destroy children, open blasphemers (as if any renounce God, deny the truth and authority of his Holy Word, rail against his blessed sacrament).'

The procedure is outlined. The superintendent is to be informed of the charge. The person charged is summoned

to the parish church to appear before the superintendent
and his assessors. If he does not appear, the penalty is to
be publicly announced the next Sunday. If he does appear, he is to be suspended until he is tried before the
magistrate. If the magistrate is negligent in his duty, the
Church itself may proceed to excommunicate. If the man
is acquitted at the magistrate's assize, the Church cannot
proceed to excommunicate. If the man is condemned, he
is excommunicated, until he has given evidence of due
repentance and faith, and then he may be granted absolution for his sin. If the man becomes a fugitive, then
the Church, acting on its own, publicly pronounces his
excommunication. Excommunication is the weapon of
the Church. 'The civil sword is in the hand of God's
magistrate: the sword granted by God to his Church is
excommunication.'

When the man expresses a desire for restoration, forty
days must pass; he will then be allowed to hear the sermon, but not the prayers before or after it. The most
serious procedure of restoration is in the case of murder,
incest, adultery and witchcraft. The procedure in the case
of a murderer is described, but essentially it is the same
for the heinous sins. The restoration of the murderer will
not be considered at all, unless he has made satisfaction
and restitution to the friends and kin of the man slain.
For three Sundays he must stand 'in a public place before
the church door, bare-footed and bare-headed, having the
same weapon which he used in the murder, or the like,
bloody in his hand'. He must make public confession of
his sin. On the last of the three Sundays, he is brought
into the church and placed in front of the pulpit. It is
certified that he has done what he was instructed to do.
The minister recites the record of his sin. The congregation is asked if it is satisfied. If it is, then his sin is pronounced to be remitted, and he is embraced as a brother.

In the case of sins which are not punishable by civil
law – fornication, habitual drunkenness, swearing, cursed

speaking, chiding, fighting, brawling, common contempt
of the order of the Church, sabbath-breaking and the like
– the person charged is called before the minister; he is
publicly rebuked in the presence of the congregation;
public satisfaction is made. If he refuses to appear before
the congregation, he is excommunicated.

In the case of less heinous offences – such as wanton
and vain words, uncomely gestures, negligence in hearing
preachings, abstaining from the Lord's Table, suspicion
of avarice or pride, superfluity or riotousness in hair or
raiment – the person charged is first privately warned by
one or two. If he is obstinate, two or three witnesses are
taken to confront him. If he responds to the rebuke, there
the matter rests. If he is obstinate, the minister and kirk
session are informed. If he acknowledges his fault, and
shows a proper penitence, no more is said about it, other
than that he is publicly warned, though not by name. If
he is still obstinate, he is warned by name. And if even
then he remains obstinate, he may be excommunicated.
It can be seen that even a small misdemeanour might
lead to excommunication, not because of itself, but because of the obstinacy of the man who committed it.

Clearly, it is of the first importance that repentance
should be sincere. To that end, Knox stressed the importance of instruction. 'For it is but one mocking to present
such to public repentance as neither understand what sin
is, what repentance is, what grace is, nor by whom God's
favour and mercy is purchased.' The penitent is therefore
publicly addressed at the Church service, after the sermon and before the prayer and the psalm.

The person charged was given three public admonitions before excommunication was pronounced. The formula for pronouncing excommunication was as follows:
'We are compelled, therefore, in view of his stubbornness,
to give the said N into the hands and power of the devil,
to the destruction of the flesh, if that by that means he
may be brought to the consideration of himself, and to

repent and avoid that fearful condemnation that shall fall on all inobedient in the day of the Lord Jesus.'

The warrant for the whole matter of excommunication Knox finds in three passages of Scripture. First, in Jesus' command that the man who will not listen to either the individual or the Church should be held as 'an ethnic (a Gentile) and a publican'. Second, the action taken by Paul in 1 Corinthians 5. Third, the command to expel the leper from among God's people. That command is just as necessary in the case of spiritual leprosy. The Church must be kept free from all infection, 'for, as it is even a work both uncharitable and cruel to join together in one bed persons infected with pestilent or other contagious and infective sores, with tender children, or with such as were whole, so it is no less cruelty to suffer amongst the flock of Jesus Christ such obstinate rebels'.

Excommunication is defined as the cutting off from the body of Jesus Christ, from participation in the sacraments, and from public prayers with his Church. The minister is in all cases to 'ask the whole Church if any think that such contempt should be suffered among them'. The final instruction is that all the faithful must hold the excommunicated person as an ethnic (a Gentile). No one must use his familiar company, yet no one must accuse him of any crime other than that of which he was convicted. Every man shall secretly call upon God for peace to be granted to the person excommunicated. So long as there is hope, the minister may talk with the person excommunicated, but, if he continues to be obstinate, 'then ought all the faithful utterly to abhor his presence and communication' – but all the more earnestly they must keep praying for him.

Such is the picture of Knox's idea of the authority and the discipline of the Church. Here again we have the high ideal of the Church's comprehensive authority, but I do not think that it is unfair to say that it lacks something of the spirit of mercy which runs through Calvin's writing on discipline. We will finally look at how this idea of discipline and authority worked practically in Scotland, where above all Knox's writ ran.

We shall first of all look at two preliminary but important matters.

We shall first look at the relationship between Church and State laid down in the Westminster Confession. Chapter 23 of the Confession deals with the position of the civil magistrate:

> The civil magistrate may not assume to himself the administration of the word and the sacraments, or the power of the keys of the kingdom of heaven: yet he hath authority, and it is his duty, to take order, that unity and peace be preserved in the Church, that the truth of God be kept pure and entire, that all blasphemies and heresies be suppressed, all corruptions and abuses in worship prevented or reformed, and all the ordinances of God duly settled, administered and observed. For the better effecting whereof, he hath power to call synods, to be present at them, and to provide that whatsoever is transacted in them be according to the mind of God. It is the duty of the people to pray for magistrates, to honour their persons, to pay them tribute and other dues, to obey their lawful commands, and to be subject to their authority for conscience' sake. Infidelity, or difference in religion, doth not make void the magistrate's just and lawful authority, nor free the people from their due obedience to him: from which ecclesiastical persons are not exempted; much less hath the Pope any power or jurisdiction over them in their dominions, or over any of their people; and least of all to deprive them of their dominions or lives, if he shall judge them to be heretics, or upon any other pretence whatsoever.

With that chapter, chapter 30, the chapter on Church Censures, very closely goes:

The Lord Jesus, as king and head of the Church, hath therein appointed a government in the hand of church-officers, distinct from the civil magistrate.

To these officers the keys of heaven are committed, by virtue whereof they have power respectively to retain and remit sins, to shut that kingdom against the impenitent both by the word and censures; and to open it unto penitent sinners, by the ministry of the gospel, and by absolution from censures, as occasion shall require.

Church censures are necessary for the reclaiming and gaining of offending brethren; for deterring of others from like offences; for purging out that leaven which might infect the whole lump; for vindicating the honour of Christ, and the holy profession of the gospel; and for preventing the wrath of God, which might justly fall upon the Church, if they should suffer his convenant, and the seals thereof, to be profaned by notorious and obstinate sinners.

For the better attaining of these ends, the officers of the Church are to proceed to admonition, suspension from the sacrament of the Lord's Supper, and by excommunication from the Church, according to the nature of the crime, and the demerit of the person.

The civil magistrate is given his place, but not more than his place. He is supreme in the civil sphere, and in ecclesiastical affairs he is the ally of the Church. The Church has distinctly kept for itself the power of 'loosing and binding', and has retained all its disciplinary powers.

The second preliminary matter is this. When we come to look at the part that the Church claimed and played in the lives of the ordinary people, we will be astonished. But T. M. Lindsay in his *History of the Reformation* points out that in any mediaeval town the civil authorities claimed rights which appear to us astonishing. In any mediaeval town there were laws about extravagance in dress, about eating and drinking, about cursing and swearing, about gaming, dancing, masquerades. The number of guests who could be invited to a wedding was laid down. The same was true of a dinner or a dance. It was laid down when the pipers were to play, when they were to leave off, and what they were to be paid. For long enough these laws and regulations might be comfortably in abeyance, but spasms of righteousness were likely to descend on a community, and then a maid-servant would be summoned for wearing a silk apron, a father for a too luxurious wedding feast, a citizen for working on a Church festival day, a mother for adorning her daughter too gaily for a wedding. As Lindsay says, municipal discipline seems to us vexatious and despotic, and there was nothing that Calvin or Knox laid down which cannot be paralleled in the rule book of any fif-teenth- or sixteenth-century municipality.

Henry Graham in *The Social Life of Scotland in the Eighteenth Century* tells of some of the things which in those days were done in the name of religion and by the authority of the Church. The kirk session of Foulis-Easter met for twelve days to discuss the case of a woman who said to another: 'Deil tak ye – Devil take you.' In the end she was severely censured. A woman who had said: 'Deil tak the skin of you and make a winnock (window) in hell with it' was excommunicated. On Sunday, Church at-tendance was compulsory and the elders went out to 'per-lustrate' the streets, to enter change-houses, to look into windows and doors of private dwellings, and to bring the deserters to kirk, or to report them to the kirk session. When the time of the evening service came the elders were on duty again to send to their homes all who were found 'vaguing', strolling, or loitering in the fields or on the roads. When a minister had a fellow-minster preach-ing for him he would take the opportunity to accompany his elders. In 1720 the minister of Forfar in one house found two persons drinking ale; in another he found a man sitting with his jacket off; in another he found a parishioner eating his dinner. The patrolling elders might even enter into any house or pry into any room. Acts of Parliament forbade barbers to shave the heads of gentlemen, or carry their periwigs to them on the Sunday. 'To carry a pail of water to the house, to fodder horses or clean their stalls, to cut kail in the yard, to grind snuff – all were offences punished without hesitation.' The minister himself was not immune; he could be suspended for having a shoulder of mutton roasted or his peruke decked on the Lord's Day.

The Presbytery of Edinburgh felt itself compelled to denounce 'the great number who took an unaccountable liberty in despising and profaning the Lord's Day idly and wickedly, by standing in companies on the streets misspending the time in idle discourse and in useless communications wholly alien to the true design of the day', as well as those who 'immediately before public worship and after it is over take recreations in walking in the fields, links, meadows, and other places, and by entering taverns, ale-houses, and milk-houses drink, tipple and otherwise spend any part thereof, or by giving or receiving social visits, or by idly gazing out of windows beholding vanities abroad – an indication not only of levity, but a profane neglect of the fittest time to salvation work'. Even the most trivial things were turned into crimes – to have carried a pair of shoes on a Fast Day, to have whistled or walked on the roads, to have pulled a turnip in the garden, even to have carried a can of water to a sick person. Even on the weekdays at nine o'clock in the evening the elders patrolled the streets to see if any loitered on the way, and entered taverns to send home anyone who was there.

Especially in the case of an illegitimate child or any report of immorality, offenders were compelled to stand 'at the pillory' – the pillory was a raised platform or stool in front of the pulpit – and to be admonished by the

minister until he was satisfied that they were truly penitent. A person might be compelled to appear ten, fifteen
or even twenty-six times, and might even have to give
'circular satisfaction' by appearing in several churches
throughout the presbytery. Such was the ordeal that some
fled the country; some even committed suicide; and many
girls killed their babies in the hope of escaping such discipline, until child murder became one of the commonest
of crimes.

Another thing which the Church had set its face
against was 'penny weddings' with their 'promiscuous
dancing'. At the time of a wedding it was the custom for
people to contribute one penny each to provide food,
drink and a fiddler. To possess a fiddle was to risk a summons to a Church court, and to have played one at a
penny wedding entailed a penalty of £20 Scots and exclusion from the Lord's Table. In 1715 the kirk session of
Morton recorded its views: 'Considering that the great
abuse that is committing at wedding dinners, and in particular by promiscuous dancing betwixt young men and
young women, which is most abominable, not to be practised in a land of light, and condemned in former times
of Presbytery as not only unnecessary but sensual, being
only an inlet of lust and provocation to uncleanness
through the corruptions of men and women in this loose
and degenerate age, wherein the devil seems to be raging
by a spirit of uncleanness and profanity, making such
practices an occasion to the flesh, and thereby drawing
men and women to dishonour God, ruin their own souls
and cast reproach upon the holy ways of religion' – considering all this the Session 'ordain that whoever shall
suffer promiscuous dancing at their bridals, either free or
penny weddings, shall forfeit three dollars, and the persons so dancing shall be rebuked before the congregation'. To the Church of those days there was something
satanic in pleasure. 'Dancing was a carnal excitement,
cards a dangerous pastime, dicing was an impious game,

... the theatre was the devil's playground, and dancing assemblies were the recruiting assemblies for Satan's ranks. Books could not be too carefully chosen, for poetry was fanciful and tales were frivolous and untrue; and such papers as the *Tatler* and *Spectator* were not fit for well-disposed minds.'

In those days the Church was claiming and exercising an authority which covered every detail in life.

Chapter 7

Authority Today

Life without authority is unthinkable and would be un-livable. Life is surrounded by authority; we live in a con-text of authority. No kind of association is possible with-out authority. Arthur Miller wrote in *The Crucible*: 'All organisation is and must be grounded on the idea of ex-clusion and prohibition, just as two objects cannot oc-cupy the same space.' If people wish to associate with each other, they have to accept certain rules, and those who will not accept the rules are necessarily excluded from the association. The association has the right to tell a man what he must do and what he must not do, and even, in some cases, what he must believe and what he must not believe, if he wishes to belong to it.

So the craftsman will live under the authority of his Trade Union, which will lay down the conditions under which he must work, and which has the right to expel him, if he will not accept and abide by these conditions. The doctor and the lawyer have their professional asso-ciations which lay down certain standards of qualifica-tion and of ethical conduct which they must observe. In politics the Scottish National Party will not accept into its membership a man who is convinced that Scotland should be governed from London; the Conservative Party will not be open to a man who believes that nationalisa-tion is the panacea for all ills any more than the Socialist Party will be open to the man who believes in the gospel of capitalism and private enterprise. If men are to associate, they must accept the conditions of association.

The matter is even more comprehensive than that. The whole business of living together in any way would be impossible without the existence and the acceptance of authority. To take a very simple example, traffic conditions would become not only difficult but suicidal, if we could not take it for granted that drivers will accept and obey the authority of the traffic lights. In a wider sense, no people could enjoy the social benefits which we enjoy, unless they were prepared to pay their taxes municipal and national. For a nation to exist authority and the acceptance of it are essential.

Authority enters into all sorts of spheres. There is the authority of convention. It would, for instance, be very difficult to run a home and care for a family, unless the members of it are prepared to accept the conventional hours of sleeping and waking and eating. Convention is a kind of lubricant to make living together possible. There are the laws of health, which a man neglects or defies at his peril. If he is to remain an efficient human being, he must accept the authority of the laws which govern his physical existence as a human being. There are the economic laws. Neither an individual or a nation can break the economic laws without ending in bankruptcy. Solvency demands obedience to economic authority.

There is a religious word which well illustrates this whole situation, the word *heresy*. The English word *heresy* is derived from the Greek word *hairesis*, which means *the act of choosing*. Heresy is the act of choosing to go one's own way in matters of belief rather accepting the position of the Church; it is the act of exalting one's private opinion above the authority of the Church.

It is interesting and significant to see how the idea of authority ever arose. Why did people come together and agree to live by certain rules? Why did they not remain individuals with no law but their own wishes and desires? An ancient writer put it this way: 'Men huddled together that they might be safe.' In coming together they sought safety from their enemies, safety in common action, safety against the strong bad man, against whom they would have been individually helpless but whom in union they were able to control. The significant thing is that men accepted the authority and the discipline involved in living together for their own welfare and for their own sake. It may well be taken as a first principle that authority is imposed and authority is accepted, not for the sake of the person who exercises it, but for the sake of the people who accept it. Authority is not the tyrant's weapon; it is the ordinary man's protection and defence. Authority is not designed to ensure the position of the big man; it is designed to protect the position of the little man. Of course, authority may be misused and abused, but it began for the defence of weakness and not for the enhancement of power.

In view of what we have said, and in the nature of the case, it is only natural that, when the Church appears as an institution, it appears as an authority-claiming and discipline-exercising society. In his *Apology* Tertullian writes: 'We are a society with a common religious feeling, unity of discipline, a common bond of hope.' He tells how the Christians meet for prayer, for scripture reading, for exhortation, and then he goes on: 'There is, besides exhortation in our gatherings, rebuke, divine censure. For judgment is passed, and it carries great weight, as it must among men certain that God sees them; and it is a notable foretaste of judgment to come, if any man has so sinned as to be banished from all share in our prayer, our assembly and all holy intercourse' (Tertullian, *Apology* 39; translated T. R. Glover). Here is the picture of a society in the habit of exercising its authority over its members.

In Hippolytus' treatise on *The Apostolic Tradition* there is a section on 'the crafts and professions forbidden to Christians'. The rule is laid down for the administrators of the Church: 'They shall enquire about the craft and occupations of those who are brought for instruction.' Of the following people it is said: 'Let him desist or be rejected' – a pander who supports harlots, a sculptor or painter who is to be taught not to make idols, an actor or one who makes shows in the theatre, a man who teaches children worldly knowledge (but if such a man has no other trade by which to live, he is to be forgiven), a charioteer or one who takes part in the games or who goes to the games, a gladiator or a trainer of gladiators, a huntsman (in the arena), or one concerned with wild beast shows or a public official concerned with gladiatorial shows, a priest or keeper of idols, a soldier, who must be instructed not to execute men even under orders, and not to take the military oath, a military governor or a city magistrate. A catechumen who wishes to become a soldier is to be cast out. A harlot or sodomite or 'one who does things which may not be spoken of' is to be rejected. A magician is not even to be considered. Charmers, astrologers, interpreters of dreams, mountebanks, makers of amulets are to be refused entry to the Church. A concubine who is a slave may be instructed, provided she has reared her children, and provided she consorts with only one man. A man who has a concubine who is a free woman must either desist or marry her legally before he can be accepted (Hippolytus, *The Apostolic Tradition* 16. 9–25).

Clearly, the early Church possessed the rights of authority and of discipline, and was prepared to use them. The modern Church still possesses these rights, and the ideals of authority and of discipline are still the same. The section on Discipline in *Practice and Procedure in the Church of Scotland* sets out the aim of discipline and lays down the methods whereby it may be exercised.

The ends contemplated by discipline are 'the glory of God, the purity of the Church, and the spiritual benefit

of members'. It is always to be administered in 'faithful-
ness, meekness, love and tenderness'. The censures avail-
able are 'admonition, rebuke, suspension, deposition
from office and excommunication'. Admonition consists
in 'addressing the offender, placing his sin or offence before him and exhorting him to greater rectitude'. This
may have to be done publicly, but there are cases when
private admonition will be suitable. Rebuke is 'a severer
form of censure involving reproof'. Suspension is a temporary exclusion from full communion and from the
other privileges of membership of the Church. It may or
may not be for a specified period, and is to be removed as
soon as sufficient cause for its removal is to be seen. Suspension from office debars from both the privileges and
the duties of office. Deposition from office consists in 'de-
priving an office-bearer of the office with which he is in-
vested', and will only be resorted to in very serious cases.
'Excommunication or exclusion from the fellowship of
the Church is resorted to only in cases of peculiar aggra-
vation, when all other means of reclaiming the offender
have failed, and when he continues impenitent and contumacious.' The proceedings and decisions of a civil
court can be no substitute for the process of discipline in
a Church court, although the decision of the civil court
will sometimes provide guidance as to whether or not the
process of discipline ought to be embarked upon. The
ideal is there and the method is there.

   In his article on Christian Discipline in Hastings'
Encyclopaedia of Religion and Ethics D. S. Schaff lays
down the reasons for discipline. 'Church discipline is that
body of measures which have been employed in the Christian Church to secure its own purity and the spiritual
well-being of its members by the punishment of offenders
against its constitution and teachings.' Discipline has a
relation to the Church. The Church is an institution
'endowed with the quality of holiness and entrusted with
the deposit of revealed truth'. It is therefore under obli-

gation to preserve itself from all that would 'taint its purity and thwart its activity in training its members and in bearing witness to the world'. Discipline equally has a relation to the individual offender. Its aim must be in the first place to reclaim him from error of doctrine or impurity of life, so that, if possible, his soul may be saved. If this should prove impossible, then the aim is 'to cut him off as a withered branch from the body of Christ', and from all participation in its benefits. T. M. Lindsay writes in *The Church and the Ministry in the Early Centuries*: 'The Church is a visible society, and the society must have, like every form of corporate social existence, powers of oversight and discipline to be exercised upon its members.'

Here then is the situation today. The need of discipline is acknowledged; the ideal of discipline is presented; the method of disciple is laid down. But the fact is that in forty years in the ministry I have never personally encountered a case of discipline; I have never had to deal with one; only on one occasion a presbytery of which I was a member had to deal with a *fama,* a report or rumour about a minister. And I find that my experience is typical, and that cases of discipline, whether in regard to moral conduct or character, or in regard to creed and belief, are so rare as to be almost non-existent. We must enquire, first, into the reasons for this situation, and, second, we must ask if it is right that the Church should very largely have abandoned the exercise of authority and discipline.

Why then is the place of discipline in the life of the Church so much smaller than once it was?

(a) The Church itself has not the place in the life of the community which once it had. It is now a minority movement. It no longer dominates public opinion. It has been estimated that fewer than one in ten people attend church on a Sunday. When people do remain attached to the Church, many of them do so as part of the respectable conventions of life rather than as part of the essence of life. One of the characters in Sean O'Casey's *The Plough and the Stars* says: 'There's no reason to bring religion into it. I think we ought to have as great a regard for religion as we can, so as to keep it out of as many things as possible.' Howard Williams, the minister of Blooms-bury Baptist Church in London, in his book on preaching *My Word* notes a very significant fact. Until a few years ago *The Sunday Times* and *The Observer* used to give some little space to the advertising of the Sunday services of a number of London Churches. Quite recently a letter went out from both of them pointing out that the increasing demand for news-space made it impossible to continue this service. Dr. Williams goes on: '*The Sunday Times* and *The Observer* now advertise as an alternative some guidance about where people can go on a Sunday in London ... The visitor to London is now offered a catho-lic and varied programme. Exhibitions, gardens, (involv-ing some slight travel and exercise), music, open air events, theatrical events, walks and pub crawls.... Are we then to assume, in 1973, that the people in London on any Sunday would not dream of looking for a place of worship?' Whatever the reason, and whatever the conclu-sion, the fact is that two serious and responsible news-papers have come to the conclusion that the Sunday ser-vices of the Church are now neither sufficiently popular or interesting to merit announcement space.

Bernard Levin, a skilled commentator on the contem-porary scene, wrote a book called *The Pendulum Years* in which he deals with 'Britain and the Sixties'. In it he has a chapter entitled 'Odium Theologicum' in which he deals with the religious situation. In that chapter he says that, while people are still married and buried in the bosom of the Church, that while they still bring their children for baptism (though much less commonly for confirmation), that while they still attend Church in some numbers at Easter, and at Christmas many a

Church is filled 'if not with the devout than at any rate with the musical', the Archbishop of Canterbury in 1969 could say: 'There is a large part of the community quite indifferent to religion.' Bernard Levin's comment is that this is an understatement of sublime dimensions: 'By the Sixties it was easier to get a camel to pass through the eye of a needle than to get men, rich or poor into the churches.'

We may like it or regret it, it remains true that no sanction that the Church could impose would make very much difference to most people nowadays. For a very large number of people it would make little or no difference if they were excluded from a communion service. The *parson* was once the *person* of the parish, but he no longer occupies that premier place.

The public would no longer stand for the kind of discipline which was exercised two hundred years ago. Public display of sorrow at the penitent's form is something which the twentieth-century man would simply refuse to accept. Even if the Church had the desire to exercise the old stern discipline, it has, as things are, neither the place nor the power to do so.

(b) This is in general a generation which resents authority. Colin MacInnes writes in *Absolute Beginners*: 'In this decade we witness the second Children's Crusade, armed with strength and booty, against all "squares", all adult nay-sayers.' This generation is againt all authority, and least of all has it any use for the authority of the Church. There is an almost total collapse of the standards in the very things for which discipline used to be imposed. In this country every thirteenth child born into the world is born out of wedlock, and in the case of babies born to girls under twenty, two out of every three are conceived out of wedlock. Things which were once regarded as shameful are greeted with no more than a shrug of vague regret. Discipline is not a conception which means much to an indisciplined age. Bernard

Levin in the book already quoted comments on the fre-
quency of outbreaks of violence in the Sixties and comments that beneath the superficial violence there was
something far deeper and something that must cause far
deeper concern: 'This was the apparent breakdown of
the inarticulate premise on which societies such as Britain's rest, namely the acceptance, in the last resort, by all
members of it, of that society's minimum standard of
authority.' Authority was fast becoming not only an un-
fashionable but even an intolerable word.

Bernard Levin in a chapter entitled 'The machine
stops' describes the change in the standards of Britain in
the Sixties: 'The abolition of capital punishment, for instance, was eventually achieved ... The reform of the
savage laws against male homosexual behaviour, repeatedly questioned and repeatedly frustrated, also went
through, with comparatively little opposition (though
that very strident) ... Not long afterwards the law on
abortion was no less radically amended, though there the
fight was more bitter and prolonged, and wild charges
continued to be flung about ... London was dubbed "the
abortion capital of the world" ... Finally, at the very end
of the decade, a new divorce Act was passed, which gave
Britain the most humane and reasonable divorce laws in
the world.'

Whether standards were improved or debased is a matter of argument; that they were different is certain; and it
is equally certain that difference was in the direction of
relaxation.

(c) Even within the Church there is less intensity of
belief. Intensity of belief tends nowadays to be rather
embarrassing than attractive. A character in Somerset
Maugham's *The Circle* says: 'I don't think you want too
much sincerity in society. It would be like an iron girder
in a house of cards.' Somehow even the Church has a fear
of being too religious. A character in Arthur Miller's *The*

Crucible says: 'There are many who stay away from church these days because you hardly ever mention God any more.' Religion is something to be played down rather than to be proudly or defiantly displayed.

As for the idea of discipline for heresy, it is becoming more and more difficult to be a heretic. Certainty is an eccentricity and doubt a virtue, and orthodoxy is almost a bad word. Sometimes we feel that the famous words of Winston Churchill about the government in his Royal Albert Hall speech in 1936 could be true of the kind of religion which is fashionable in the Church: 'So they go on in strange paradox, decided only to be undecided, resolved to be irresolute, adamant for drift, solid for fluidity, all-powerful for impotence.'

It is a strange thing to think of the one time 'fundamentals'. *The Fundamentals* consisted originally of a series of twelve small volumes, published between 1909 and 1915 which expounded the basic beliefs of the Christian faith. These basic beliefs were five – the inspiration and the infallibility of the Bible; the personal deity of Jesus Christ with the Virgin Birth as the witness and guarantee of it; the substitutionary atonement; the physical resurrection of Christ; and his personal return. It is no exaggeration to say that a man could now well claim to be a member of the Church without believing in a single one of these five beliefs. Discipline for heresy would be very difficult when there has ceased to be any such thing as heresy.

I knew a man with a very acute mind, and a very real but very unorthodox faith. There was a time when the Church of Scotland seemed set to revise its creed. One would have thought that my friend would have welcomed credal revision. But no; his reaction was: 'Don't let them make a new creed; they'll expect us to believe in it!' He meant that a man could interpret and understand the old creeds much as he liked – and he liked it that way. He did not want to be bound by a definite statement of belief. And that may well be true of a large part of the Church today.

Bernard Levin in the chapter on '*Odium theologicum*' harks back to the publication of John Robinson's *Honest to God* in 1963. John Robinson was then Bishop of Woolwich. 'It is not every day,' said the *Church Times* in an editorial, 'that a bishop goes on public record as apparently denying almost every Christian doctrine of the Church in which he holds office.' 'Everywhere,' comments Bernard Levin on the Sixties. 'men longed for a scientific form of myth, a non-compulsory set of commandments, an undivine God.' 'The bishop, emboldened, agreed to write a series of articles for the *Sunday Pictorial*, in which he briskly disposed of Adam and Eve, the Virgin Birth, Life after Death, the Resurrection ("Next Sunday: Did Christ really rise from the tomb?") and the Miracles; further emboldened, he declared that "Regarded as a code of conduct, the Sermon on the Mount is quite impractical," on the grounds that it "tears the individual loose from any horizontal nexus".'

Not only were the Christian creeds under attack from within the Church; orthodox Christian morality is also attacked. John Robinson spoke of 'The new Morality'. The new morality is largely Joseph Fletcher's situation ethic, of which the basic principle is that there is nothing which can be labelled absolutely good or absolutely bad. Its quality depends on the situation. Suppose, for instance, that a man is sexually a menace to small girls. Suppose that he can be persuaded to engage in sexual intercourse in the normal way, whether by means of adultery or fornication, with a prostitute, with an unmarried woman, or with someone else's wife. Then suppose that involvement in such normal sexual experience frees him from his abnormal sexual desires, then, so the argument runs, the adultery or the fornication is a good thing. As Bernard Levin remembers, Canon Douglas

Rhymes wrote his book *No New Morality*. His aim was to find a new basis for sexual morality. He abandoned most of the traditional points of view and concluded that 'sex is good and enjoyable if it serves the fulfilment of man as a total being'.

Authority must be a diminishing force in a society in which it is next to impossible to be a heretic, and in which what was once immorality has become morality.

(d) It is unfortunately true that for many people the Church has a bad image. For some, all religion is little more than a last lingering relic of superstition. Doris Langley Moore said in *The Vulgar Heart*: 'The Churches grow old but they do not grow up.' It is as if to say that religion, at least the Church's religion, belongs to the childhood of the race, and is only for the childish in mentality. H. L. Mencken in *Minority Report* is even more sweeping: 'The scientist who yields anything to theology, however slight, is yielding to ignorance, and false pretences, and as certainly as if he granted that a horse-hair put into a bottle of water will turn into a snake.' In a statement like that it is the assumption that the beliefs of religion are a mixture of ignorance and superstition.

Nor has the old idea that religion takes the joy out of life wholly died. Again to quote Mencken: 'The chief contribution of Protestantism to human thought is the massive proof that God is a bore.' And Dorothy Parker writes in *Partial Comfort*:

> Whose love is given over-well
> Shall look on Helen's face in hell,
> Whilst they whose love is thin and wise
> May view John Knox in paradise.

Doubtless the idea that religion is to be ranked with the fairy tales of childish superstition and the idea that it drains life of its colour and its vitality are both mistaken and unjustified, but those who hold these ideas are not likely to accept the authority of a religion which no intelligent man will accept and which no one in love with life will tolerate.

(e) But there are reasons for the departure from discipline which in their own way are good reasons. There is what might be called a greater humility; there is much less wish to stand in judgment over our fellowmen than once there was. In the days, for instance, in Scotland when discipline was widely and sternly dealt out, the elders, the kirk session,-found a certain joy and satisfaction in the task of sitting in judgment. There is little of that spirit in the modern Church. Rather, if someone errs, we are much more willing to say: 'There but for the grace of God go I.' We are much more reluctant to throw the first stone (John 8. 7). We are conscious of the truth in Edward Wallis Hoch's often quoted words:

> There is so much good in the worst of us,
> And so much bad in the best of us,
> That it hardly becomes any of us
> To talk about the rest of us.

We are not so sure nowadays about the right of any man to sit in moral judgment on any other man. The answer would be that, when the Church exercises authority and when the Church imposes discipline, those who have the task of doing so do so not in their own right but as representatives of the Church, that, so to speak, there is nothing personal in this. But even at that people are much less willing to judge than once they were. If that hesitancy comes from no more than the easy tolerance which is born of slack indifference, it is a dangerous thing. But if it is born of a genuine humility, then Christian discipline may become the act of Christian love rather than of ecclesiastical power.

(f) Another awareness has entered into the situation, the awareness that there are many cases in which an unpunishable sin is very much more serious than the other

scandal which would once have received discipline. Is a
man whose marriage ends in divorce more deserving of
censure or a man whose marriage continues, but who by
his selfishness or worse has made life a hell for his wife? Is
the man who makes a mistake in a moment of impulse or
passion, a mistake whose consequences can be seen, so
much more deserving of discipline than the man who,
coldly respectable, makes no such mistake, but makes life
intolerable for his family or his employees? It can often
be the case that the man who has, so to speak, no public
sins, is guilty of private conduct which does at least as
much, and perhaps more, damage. There can be an arrogance, a selfishness, an insensitiveness, a conscious or un-
conscious cruelty which are beyond the power of discipline to touch but which are worse than the open sin.
The consequences of this awareness is that people are less
willing and less quick to impose discipline on others, for
they know very well that there are worse things hidden
from sight under a façade of apparent faultlessness.

There are bad reasons and there are good reasons for
being less critical – and both kinds enter into this case.

Where then does this bring us in regard to the exercise
of authority and the imposing of discipline in the Church
today? We must begin by laying down certain basic
principles.

i. There is about the Church a certain paradox. In the
first place, the Church exists for the sake of sinners. If the
Church was a place for perfect people, there would be no
Church. 'I came,' said Jesus, 'not to call the righteous, but
sinners' (Matthew 9. 13; Mark 2. 17; Luke 5. 32). 'Him
who comes to me,' said Jesus, 'I will not cast out' (John 6.
37). The Church is the place to which the sinner is invited to come.

'Rabbi' Duncan was one of the most famous of Scottish
preachers. It is told that at a Communion Service, when
he offered the cup to a woman, she hesitated to take it,
and it was obvious that her hesitation came from the feel-

ing of unworthiness. Whereat 'Rabbi' Duncan said to her gently: 'Take it woman; it's for sinners; it's for you.' Epictetus used to speak of the teachings of philosophy as 'medicine for the sick soul'. It was the sick soul that the philosopher was out to help and heal. No one could criticise a Church for being full of sinners any more than he could criticise a doctor because his surgery was full of sick people. The doctor's surgery is the very place to which a sick person ought to go, and the more sick people who throng to him, the better a doctor he must be.

So the first arm of the paradox is that the Church is the place for sinners.

ii. But in the second place, the Church is the place for the people whom the New Testament calls saints. It is always to the saints in this or that town that Paul addresses his letters (Romans 1. 7; 1 Corinthians 1. 2; 2 Corinthians 1. 1; Ephesians 1. 1; Philippians 1. 1; Colossians 1. 2). Jesus is depicted as offering men the new birth, the origin of which is not human but divine, and of insisting on the necessity of that birth (John 1. 13; 3. 3). When Jesus healed or forgave a person, he more than once added the warning that that person must be done with sin. He said to the paralysed man at the pool after he had healed him: 'See, you are well! Sin no more, that nothing worse befall you' (John 5. 14). He said to the woman taken in adultery, after he had forgiven her and saved her from the self-righteous fury of the crowd: 'Go, and do not sin again' (John 8. 11). Jesus dealt most gently with sinners, but he was very far from saying that sin does not matter.

We meet the paradox head on in Romans 6. 'Are we to continue in sin that grace may abound?' (Romans 6. 1). There were people who said to Paul: 'You say that God's grace is great enough to forgive anything?' 'Yes.' 'You say that God's grace is the most wonderful thing in the world?' 'Yes.' 'Then,' they argued, 'let's go on sinning, for, the more we sin, the more there will be of this wonderful grace. Sin is a good thing, because sin produces grace.' But Paul is clear that a man dies with Christ in baptism so that his sinful body may be destroyed and he may no longer be enslaved to sin. The Christian must consider himself dead to sin. Sin must no longer reign in his mortal body. Sin must have no more dominion over him (Romans 6. 5–14). Grace is not given to enable a man to go on being a sinner; it is given to him to stop him being a sinner. Paul writes to the Corinthians: 'Do you not know that the unrighteous will not inherit the king-dom of God? Do not be deceived; neither the immoral, nor idolaters, nor sexual perverts, nor thieves, nor the greedy, nor drunkards, nor revilers, nor robbers will in-herit the kingdom of God. And such were some of you. But you were washed, you were sanctified, you were justified in the name of the Lord Jesus and in the Spirit of our God' (1 Corinthians 6. 9–11). If the Church is the place for sinners, it is also very much the place for saints.

Nowhere does this paradox meet us more vividly than in the First Letter of John. John writes near the begin-ning of the Letter: 'If we say we have no sin, we deceive ourselves, and the truth is not in us' (1 John 1. 8), which amounts to a statement that no man is without sin. But later in the Letter John also writes: 'Everyone who commits sin is guilty of lawlessness. You know that he appeared to take away sins, and in him there is no sin. No one who abides in him sins; no one who sins has either seen him or known him. Little children, let no one de-ceive you. He who does right is righteous, as he is righte-ous. He who commits sin is of the devil; for the devil has sinned from the beginning. The reason the son of God appeared was to destroy the works of the devil. No one born of God commits sin; for God's nature abides in him, and he cannot sin because he is born of God' (1 John 3. 4–9). Here in the one Letter John insists first that that there is no one who has not sinned, and second that no one who is born of God can sin.

The explanation of the paradox is not difficult. The

Church is the place for sinners, but it is not the place for those who are content or determined to remain sinners. There are two kinds of sinners. There is the man who sins because he is swept away in a moment's passion, defeated by a moment's weakness, and who having sinned, is truly and deeply sorry for what he has done, who knows bitterly what guilt and shame are. And there is the man who sins obstinately, defiantly, deliberately, the man who knows what he is doing, who is not sorry for what he has done, and who has no intention of ceasing to do it. Numbers 15. 22–31 lays down the ways in which atonement may be made for the man who has sinned. But again and again it is laid down that such atonement is for the man who has sinned *unwittingly*. No sacrifice avails for the man who has done anything *with a high hand*. The man who knowingly, purposefully, defiantly sins and continues to sin is in a different kind of position.

Let us return to our analogy of the doctor's surgery. We said that it was entirely natural for a doctor's surgery to be filled with sick people. But if none of the people in the surgery get any better, if they remain as sick as ever they were, then there is something wrong with them as patients and with the doctor as a doctor. The one aim in coming to the surgery was not to stay ill but to get well.

So the Church is the place for sinners, but not for sinners who are determined to remain sinners, not for the obstinate sinner, who has no regret for his sins, and no intention other than to remain in them. It is not that such people should be debarred from the Church; but that they should be allowed to claim full membership of the Church is another question. Clearly, there is a place within the Church for the exercise of authority and the imposing of discipline.

iii. There are two other general considerations which must be taken into account. Whether we like it or not, the Church has a public image. The New Testament was well aware of that, and accepted it as an important fact. It is Peter's demand to his people: 'Maintain good conduct among the Gentiles, so that in case they speak against you as wrong-doers, they may see your good deeds, and glorify God on the day of visitation ... It is God's will that by doing right you should put to silence the ignorance of foolish men' (1 Peter 2. 12, 15). In the Pastoral Epistles, as we have already noted, one of the qualifications for the bishop is that 'he must be well thought of by outsiders' (1 Timothy 3. 7). This is to say that the Church cannot and must not disregard the impression that it is making on the outsider through the conduct of its members.

This is where the meaning of the word *saint*, as the New Testament uses it, becomes important. The word is *hagios*. We have already noted the significance of this word. It is the word which is oftenest translated *holy*; and the basic meaning is *different*. The Sabbath day is holy, because it is different from other days; the Lord's Table is holy, because it is different from ordinary tables. If the Christian is to be a saint, he must therefore be *different*. And indeed the outsider may well ask what is the point of being a member of the Church, if it makes no difference? If the people inside the Church are exactly the same as the people outside the Church, wherein lies the point of Church membership? Unless the Church member displays in his life and actions a stricter honesty, a greater diligence. a more gracious kindness, a greater ability to forgive, a greater reliability, a wider sense of responsibility, a greater selflessness, a purer sexual life, a finer ability to handle personal relationships, a greater self-discipline, a greater self-control in pleasure, what is the point of it all? If being a Christian makes no difference, why bother being a Christian? If there is no difference between the standards of the Christian and the standards of the world, then the world may well conclude that it can do very well without Christianity.

There is further the fact that the Church member is a pledged man. The Church member has partaken of the *sacrament* of the Lord's Supper. The word sacrament has more than one meaning; but its simplest meaning comes from the fact that it is derived from the Latin word *sacramentum*, which means *a soldier's oath of loyalty*, the oath, the pledge which the Roman soldier took to be ever loyal and obedient to his Emperor and his general. Therefore to come to the Lord's Table is by that very action to take an oath of loyalty to Jesus Christ.

The outsider knows perfectly well who is a Church member, and the outsider will judge the Church by the conduct of its members. The Church therefore cannot regard with indifference and unconcern conduct in its members which injures the public image of the Church.

iv. But there is something to be said about the individual as well. Nothing could have a worse effect on the individual than that he should arrive at a stage, at which he has reached the conclusion that he can get away with anything, that he has unlimited licence to do as he likes. If this happens a false freedom will beget a licence which can end in nothing but degeneration. Human nature is such that we tend to abandon standards which we are not compelled to maintain; and nothing could do more harm to the individual than for the Church to give him the impression that wrong-doing does not matter.

We have now arrived at the really difficult part of the matter. It is easy enough to analyse the situation, to describe the principles and the necessity of authority and discipline within the Church, to understand how the exercise of authority and discipline has become less and less, to lay down the reasons why authority and discipline are needed. It is much more difficult to set out the practice of discipline, the things which should be subject to discipline and the way in which discipline should be exercised. There are two areas into which the exercise of discipline enters, the area of conduct and the area of belief.

We begin with the area of conduct. There are certain things with which the ordinary law of the land deals, and anyone guilty of them undergoes the penalties and punishments which the law lays down. Violence, theft, dishonesty, debt, cruelty, drunkenness, immorality, indecency – these are things which the law of the land will punish. The First Letter of Peter is well aware that the Christian will suffer at the hands of the law as a Christian, but it lays it down that he must not suffer as a murderer, a thief or a wrong-doer (1 Peter 4. 15). The Church cannot remain indifferent and unconcerned about the things which the ordinary rules of society condemn and punish. We are not forgetting what we have already said, that there are many faults for which the law has no penalty. Malicious gossip, which murders a person's good name, trouble-making, which ruins personal relationships, violence of temper, which makes a person impossible to live with, the cruelty of tongue, which wounds the spirit, the infidelity, which breaks the heart – these things the law cannot touch. It is easy enough to discipline the person who had been divorced, but what of the person, who has done nothing which the law can touch, but whose selfishness and cruelty in personal relationships has turned a marriage into an agony?

This is frankly to admit that no system of law or discipline is or can be perfect, but this does not mean that what can be done should not be done. Another problem arises. The exercise of discipline is more difficult in some Churches than in others. Suspension from the Sacrament of the Lord's Supper will mean much more in a Church which is characteristically sacramental, and where the Communion is the essence of every service, than it will in a Church in which the Sacrament of the Lord's Supper is observed only once every three or six months. Suspension will mean much more in a Church in which the sacraments are held to convey grace by the very partaking of them than in a Church in which the main emphasis is on the sacrament as a memorial. Discipline will be easier to exercise in a Church whose priests convey absolution to its confessing members than in a Church in which there is no such practice. What then is to be done? Of what is the exercise of discipline to consist? There are four possibilities, and one general principle.

1. There is the possibility of personal and private admonition. It is in this way that the things which no law can deal with may be dealt with. This personal and private admonition would best be carried out by the minister of the congregation in the exercise of his pastoral concern. In this case none need know of it except the pastor. His admonition would be given not in criticism but in love, and the person concerned would be not only talked to but also prayed with. This is indeed not so much a thing of discipline as it is of pastoral care. I am sure that it is often done, and done with Christlike concern. But it may be that the pastor of the congregation should be encouraged to exercise his pastoral office with a greater authority and love combined. Only when he comes as the representative of Jesus Christ, and only when he brings Jesus Christ with him, will he avoid appearing no more than an interfering critic, and appear really as the pastor who bears his people on his heart.

2. There is the possibility of public and official rebuke. Just as the private admonition of pastoral concern is for the faults which are private, so the public rebuke must be kept for faults which are public, and which have brought discredit on the good name of the whole Church. I do not mean rebuke in the presence of the whole congregation when I speak of public rebuke. Nowadays congregations are so widely scattered, and very often their members are so little acquainted with each other, that rebuke in the face of the congregation would no longer have the character of an act within a fellowship. I mean by public rebuke in presence of the Kirk Session, or other governing body of the congregation, or at least by representa-

tives of that body. Further, it would be necessary to announce the fact that such rebuke had been administered. Justice must not only be done but also must be seen to be done. And one of the main aims of the whole matter is to make it clear that the Church does not regard it as unimportant when some professing member is guilty of some public fault.

3. There is the possibility of temporary suspension from the Lord's Table, suspension until the person involved has shown genuine penitence and amendment of his ways.

4. There is the possibility of complete rejection from membership of the Church, until in penitence of heart and amendment of life the person involved shall have asked for readmission into the fellowship of the Church. Such a course would be taken only in the case of an obstinate, defiant, deliberate and blatant wrong-doer, who by his attitude has already made it clear that he has no interest and in no respect for the teaching and the beliefs of the Church.

5. In no case, not even the last, is the abandonment of the person involved suggested. In no case ought he to be barred from the ordinary services of the Church. The Church door must always be open to him. The pastoral care and concern of the Church for him so far from being abandoned must be intensified. Even if he has rejected the Church, the Church cannot and must not reject him. The aim must always be to bring the lost son back.

So much then for matters of conduct; let us now turn to matters of belief. Here indeed, as we have seen, there is difficulty, for there is hardly any article of belief which has not been questioned by even the leaders of the Church. But there are necessary limits beyond which the questioning cannot go. What we call ourselves is Christians and what we claim to believe in is Christianity. This is to say that the centre of the whole matter is in an attitude to Jesus Christ. What must that attitude be? If

we like to put it so, what is the irreducible minimum of
belief about Jesus Christ?

A long time ago now I was taught theology in Trinity
College, Glasgow, which was then one of the training
schools of the United Free Church of Scotland; the professor of Systematic Theology was the well-loved A. B.
Macaulay. A. B. Macaulay once told me of a statement of
faith, which I think that he had constructed himself, and
which he used for the admission of first communicants in
his days as a parish minister. I used it in turn all through
my own ministry. It runs as follows:

> I come to the Lord's Table in obedience to the invi-
> tation and command of Jesus Christ who suffered and
> died for me.
>
> To him I owe the assurance that my sins are for-
> given.
>
> Through him I know that God is my heavenly
> Father.
>
> On him alone I depend for strength and grace to
> overcome evil and to do the right.
>
> Within this fellowship and with all his followers I
> will strive to maintain his honour upon earth.

That statement seems to me to lay down the essentials
of belief about Jesus Christ. It lays down the following
beliefs:

(a) The belief that Jesus is a real person, and not a
figure in a myth or a fairy-tale.

(b) The belief that through what Jesus did in his life
and in his death my whole relationship to God is
changed. This statement wisely does not lay down any
theory of how that happened; it insists only that it did
happen.

(c) The belief in the risen and living Christ, for if I
depend on him for strength and grace, he is no dead figure in a book, whom I remember; he is a living person
whom I experience.

(d) The belief in the Church in the fellowship of which I must live a life that is lived for Jesus Christ.

I do not think that a man can believe less than that and call himself a Christian, and to be honest, unless a man could agree to that, I would not accept him as a member of the Christian Church.

There remains one thing to say. In New Testament times two classes of Gentiles were attached to the Jewish synagogues. There were the God-fearers, who were attracted by the Jewish belief in one God as contrasted with the many gods of paganism, and who preferred the purity of the Jewish ethic to the looseness of heathen living. And there were the proselytes proper, Gentiles who had gone the whole way, who had accepted not only the Jewish view of God and the Jewish ethic, but who had also submitted to circumcision and had taken upon themselves total obedience to the Law. I think that just as there was a two-tier approach to Judaism, there is a case for a two-tier membership of the Church. There is a place for those who are deeply attracted by Jesus Christ and the Christian way, and there is a place for the many fewer who are prepared to make a total commitment to Jesus Christ. And for such a committed minority the authority and the discipline of the Church would be no formality, but a reality which they would be pledged and willing to accept. As for the uncommitted majority, they would in no sense be second-rate citizens; the Church would welcome them; the Church would hope that they would in due time make the transmission to the committed; but from them the Church would ask no more than they were prepared to give, while from the committed minority it would ask – and receive – all they had to give.